Frozen Treats
& Summer Sweets

From Coolers to Cobblers, Perfect Summer Recipes!

Printed in the United States of America
by G&R Publishing Co.

Distributed By:

507 Industrial Street
Waverly, IA 50677

ISBN-13: 978-1-56383-302-1
ISBN-10: 1-56383-302-6
Item #7092

Table of Contents

*Chill Out this Summer
with 161 Recipes to
Beat the Heat!*

3

When summer rolls around, get prepared to beat the heat with this collection of tasty frozen treats and light fruity sweets. And, in case you need a reason to indulge, here are just a few to keep you celebrating all summer long!

Official and Un-Official Summer Holidays

MAY

3rd and 4th	Dandelion Days
5th	Cinco de Mayo
1st Friday	No Pants Day
2nd Week	National Family Week
11th	Eat What You Want Day
2nd Sunday	Mother's Day
15th	National Chocolate Chip Day
16th	National Pizza Party Day
4th Monday	Memorial Day

JUNE

2nd	Leave the Office Early Day
6th and 7th	Donut Days
7th and 8th	Banana Split Days
14th	Flag Day
19th	Recess At Work Day
3rd Sunday	Father's Day
23rd	Let It Go Day
26th	National Bomb Pop Day

JULY

National Grilling Month

3rd	Stay Out Of The Sun Day
4th	Independence Day
5th	Cherry Pit Spitting Day
7th	Chocolate Day
10th	Don't Step On A Bee Day
12th	Hot Dog Day
3rd Week	Sports Cliché Week
23rd	Gorgeous Grandma Day
27th	Parents' Day

AUGUST

1st	Girlfriends' Day
1st Sunday	Friendship Day
8th	The Date To Create
8th	Sneak Some Zucchini Onto Your Neighbor's Porch Night
15th	National Best Friends' Day
16th	Sandcastle Day
4th Sunday	International Kitchen Garden Day
24th	National Waffle Day
30th	National Toasted Marshmallow Day

Frozen Favorites

Yogurt Freezies

Makes 8 popsicles

½ C. sugar-free lemon-flavored drink mix

2½ C. water

1 (6 oz.) carton strawberry yogurt

Combine drink mix and water; stir until the drink mix is completely dissolved. Stir in strawberry yogurt until well combined. Pour mixture into popsicle molds and freeze until firm.

Drip-Free Black Cherry Popsicles

Makes 8 popsicles

1 (3 oz.) box dry black cherry gelatin mix

1 (.13 oz.) env. black cherry-flavored drink mix

1 C. sugar

⅔ C. hot water

2 C. cold water

In a large pitcher, combine gelatin mix, drink mix, sugar and hot water; stir until gelatin and drink mixes are completely dissolved. Stir in cold water, then pour into popsicle molds; freeze until firm.

Strawberry Orangesicles

Makes 6 to 8 popsicles

2 C. orange juice

1 C. chopped fresh
  strawberries

1½ T. sugar

½ C. vanilla yogurt

In a blender, combine orange juice, strawberries, sugar and yogurt; blend to desired consistency. Pour mixture into popsicle molds and freeze until firm.

FLOWER POWER!

You always knew it was true, but now scientific studies have confirmed that flowers make people happy. Pick a bouquet of cheerful flowers for a loved one, or brighten your own day by filling a vase with colorful summer flowers.

Orange Dream Bars

Makes 6 to 8 popsicles

1 (6 oz.) can frozen
orange juice concentrate

1 (6 oz.) can cold water

2 C. vanilla ice cream or
frozen yogurt, softened

In a blender, combine orange juice concentrate, water and ice cream; process until well blended. Pour mixture into popsicle molds and freeze until firm. For a variation, grape or cranberry juice concentrate can be used in place of the orange juice concentrate.

Fizzy Peach Pops

Makes 6 to 8 popsicles

1 (12 oz.) can peach
or apricot nectar

1 (12 oz.) can lemon-
lime soda

1 C. crushed ice

In a pitcher, combine peach nectar, soda and crushed ice; mix well. Pour mixture into popsicle molds and freeze until firm. The crushed ice will help the popsicles retain a sparkly look.

BREAKING THE MOLD

If you do not have popsicle molds, small plastic or paper cups can do the job. Empty yogurt containers or 5-ounce paper bathroom cups are ideal. Fill the containers with liquid and place in the freezer for 1 hour. Press popsicle sticks, wooden craft sticks or plastic spoons into the slightly frozen mixture, then return to the freezer until completely frozen. Gently pry off or tear away the container, then enjoy your frozen treat!

Rocky Road Pops

Makes 8 popsicles

1 (5.9 oz.) box instant chocolate pudding mix

3 C. cold 1% or 2% milk

½ C. miniature marshmallows

¼ C. chopped peanuts, optional

In a large bowl, combine pudding mix and milk; beat with a wire whisk for 2 minutes. Fold in marshmallows and nuts. Pour mixture into popsicle molds and freeze until firm.

Pineapple Popsicles

Makes 6 to 8 popsicles

1 (8 oz.) can pineapple chunks, drained

2 C. white grape juice

1 (11 oz.) can mandarin oranges, drained

In a blender, combine pineapple chunks, mandarin oranges and grape juice; process until well blended. Pour mixture into popsicle molds and freeze until firm.

CHILL OUT

To prevent adding more heat and humidity to your home during hot summer months, schedule activities that require hot water, such as washing dishes or clothes, for early morning or late evening.

Fruit Punch Freezies

Makes 8 popsicles

3 C. fruit punch

2 T. lemon juice

1 (14 oz.) can sweetened
  condensed milk

In a pitcher, combine fruit punch, sweetened condensed milk and lemon juice; whisk together until smooth. Pour mixture into popsicle molds and freeze until firm.

Marble Pops

Makes 16 to 18 popsicles

1 (3.4 oz.) box instant
  vanilla pudding mix

1 (3.9 oz.) box instant
  chocolate pudding mix

2 C. cold milk

2 C. cold chocolate milk

2 bananas, peeled and
  mashed

1 C. miniature semi-
  sweet chocolate chips

In a large bowl, combine vanilla pudding mix and milk; beat with a wire whisk for 2 minutes. Fold in bananas; set aside. In a separate bowl, combine chocolate pudding mix and chocolate milk; beat with a wire whisk for 2 minutes. Fold in chocolate chips. Divide the vanilla mix among the popsicle molds; top each with the chocolate mix. Use a knife to swirl the two mixtures together in each mold. Freeze until firm.

GOING TO MARKET

You know it's summer when those open-air farmers' markets come to town. Contact your Chamber of Commerce for dates and times of upcoming markets. It's always good to support local farmers, and markets are a great place to purchase home-grown fruits, vegetables, baked goods and craft items.

Root Beer Float Freeze Pops

Makes 8 popsicles

1 C. vanilla ice cream   2 to 3 C. root beer

Spoon some of the ice cream into each popsicle mold. Slowly pour root beer over ice cream in each mold. The root beer will fizz a little. Once most of the fizz dies down, transfer the filled mold to the freezer; freeze until firm.

Mango Ice

Makes 1 quart

2 fresh mangoes or
  papayas or 1 (26 oz.)
  jar sliced mango or
  papaya

1 C. sugar
1 C. warm water
2 T. lemon juice

If using fresh fruit, peel, seed and cut up the mangoes or papayas. If using canned fruit, drain well. In a 2-cup measuring glass, combine the sugar and warm water, stirring until the sugar is completely dissolved. In a blender or food processor, combine half of the sugar water, half of the fruit and half of the lemon juice; process until smooth and transfer blended mixture to a 2-quart ice cream freezer or 5 x 9″ loaf pan. Repeat with remaining ingredients; transfer to same container. Cover and freeze for 4 to 5 hours or until almost firm. Transfer to a chilled mixing bowl; beat at medium speed for 2 minutes or until fluffy. Return to cold pan; cover and freeze for 6 hours or until firm.

Grape Sherbet

Makes 1 gallon

1 (14 oz.) can sweetened
  condensed milk
2 C. heavy cream
3 C. sugar

4 C. grape juice
Juice of 3 lemons
Whole milk

In a gallon-size container from an ice cream machine, combine sweetened condensed milk, cream, sugar, grape juice and lemon juice. Pour in enough whole milk until liquid reaches the container's fill line. Follow manufacturer's directions for freezing.

Apple Sorbet

Makes 4 servings

1¼ lbs. Granny Smith apples, cored and roughly chopped

¾ C. sugar
1 C. water, divided
1 C. apple juice or cider

In a medium saucepan over medium heat, combine apples, sugar and ½ cup water. Cover and cook until apples are tender, about 10 minutes. Press mixture through a sieve into a large bowl, discarding any apple skin. Stir in apple juice and another ½ cup water. Pour into an ice cream machine and follow manufacturer's directions for freezing. Or, pour into a shallow container and freeze for 6 hours, scraping with a fork every 1 or 2 hours to break up ice crystals.

THE SKIN-NY ON SUNSCREEN

When it comes to your skin, don't skimp! Purchase a high-quality sunscreen that shields you from the sun's harmful rays, but doesn't contain any harmful ingredients. Avoid sunscreens containing alcohol, fragrances, preservatives, para-aminobenzoic acid (PABA) or benzophenones. In addition, use a daily moisturizer that contains SPF. Finally, wash and re-hydrate your skin with a gentle cleanser and nourishing moisturizer after a day in the sun.

Watermelon Granita

Makes 4 servings

4 C. seedless watermelon chunks

½ C. sugar

Juice of 1 lemon

In a blender, combine watermelon, sugar and lemon juice; process until smooth. Pour mixture into a shallow container and freeze for 6 hours, scraping with a fork every 1 or 2 hours to break up ice crystals.

Key Lime Sorbet

Makes 1½ quarts

1 C. sugar

1 C. Key lime preserves

4 C. lime-flavored club soda, divided

Juice and zest of 1 lemon

Juice and zest of 1 lime

In a medium saucepan over low heat, combine sugar, preserves and 1 cup club soda; heat and stir until sugar and preserves are melted. Stir in juice and zest of lemon and lime. Slowly stir in remaining club soda. Transfer blended mixture to a 2-quart ice cream freezer or 5 x 9″ loaf pan. Cover and freeze for 4 to 5 hours or until almost firm. Transfer to a chilled mixing bowl; beat at medium speed for 2 minutes or until fluffy. Return to cold pan; cover and freeze for 6 hours or until firm.

Icy Espresso Freeze

Makes 4 servings

2 C. brewed espresso

⅓ C. plus 1 T. sugar,
  divided

½ C. heavy cream

1 T. almond liqueur, such
  as Frangelico

In a large bowl, combine espresso and ⅓ cup sugar; stir until sugar is completely dissolved. Pour mixture into a shallow container and freeze for 6 hours, scraping with a fork every 1 or 2 hours to break up ice crystals. Before serving, whip together cream, remaining 1 tablespoon sugar and liqueur until stiff peaks form. To serve, scoop frozen mixture into bowls and top each serving with a dollop of the sweetened cream.

Pineapple Carrot Frozen Delight

Makes 9 servings

3 C. baby carrots

2 C. pineapple-orange
  juice

1 T. lemon juice

½ tsp. ground ginger

¼ C. sugar

3 T. pineapple preserves

1 (8 oz.) can crushed
  pineapple in heavy
  syrup

½ C. sour cream

1 tsp. vanilla extract

In a large saucepan over medium-high heat, combine carrots, pineapple-orange juice, lemon juice, ginger and sugar; bring to a boil. Reduce heat, cover and let simmer for 20 minutes or until carrots are tender. Transfer mixture to a blender. Add preserves and pineapple with syrup; process until completely smooth, about 3 minutes. Add sour cream and vanilla; process until well blended. Pour mixture into a 9″ square pan; cover and freeze until firm, about 8 hours.

FAIR FARE

When planning your summer vacation, don't forget about a fun, affordable trip to the State Fair! Whether it's a romantic weekend escape or a getaway for the whole family, State Fairs have many exciting exhibits, demonstrations, concerts, contests, rides and live animals, not to mention a never-ending supply of foods on a stick.

Mandarin Orange Frozen Dessert

Makes 9 servings

½ C. butter

1¼ C. flour

¼ C. sugar

2 T. brown sugar

½ C. chopped walnuts

4 C. orange sherbet, softened

2 C. vanilla ice cream, softened

⅓ C. shredded coconut, toasted*

Melt butter in a large skillet over medium heat. Stir in flour, sugar, brown sugar and walnuts. Cook, stirring constantly, for 4 to 5 minutes or until mixture is golden brown. Spoon mixture into a 9" square pan; press into pan using the back of a spoon. Set aside to cool completely. Place sherbet and ice cream in a large bowl; stir gently to marble. Spread mixture over cooled crust. Top with toasted coconut. Cover and freeze for 3 to 4 hours or until firm.

* *To toast, place shredded coconut in a single layer on a baking sheet. Bake at 350° for approximately 8 minutes or until coconut is golden brown.*

YOUR #1 FAN

*Use ceiling fans and portable floor fans
to move air around within your home.
In a home without air conditioning,
fans are essential for cooling. In a home with
air conditioning, fans can move
cool air from room to room,
and allow you to raise the
thermostat setting
without affecting comfort.*

Rainbow
Sandwich Treats

Makes 20 treats

1 (18 oz.) pkg.
  refrigerated sugar
  cookie dough

½ C. flour

2 tsp. milk

4 tsp. coarse sugar or
  1 tsp. granulated sugar

1 (1.75 qt.) carton
  rainbow or tropical
  fruit sherbet

Preheat oven to 350°. In a mixing bowl, knead together cookie dough and flour. Roll out half the dough into a 10 x 14″ rectangle; cut into 2 x 3″ squares. Repeat with remaining dough. Place dough rectangles on ungreased baking sheets; prick with a fork. Brush the milk over the dough and sprinkle with sugar. Bake for 6 to 7 minutes or until the edges are lightly browned; remove from oven and cool completely. Remove carton from sherbet. Cut sherbet block in half lengthwise and then cut crosswise into 1″ slices. Cut each slice in half to make 20 slices; place on a baking sheet in a single layer and return to freezer for 1 hour. Assemble sandwiches by placing one sherbet slice between two cookies. Wrap sandwiches individually in plastic wrap; freeze for 1 to 2 hours or until firm.

Easy Ice Cream Sandwiches

Makes 15 treats

2 C. vanilla ice cream,
slightly softened

½ C. chopped peanuts,
chocolate chips or
miniature marshmallows

30 soft and chewy
chocolate chip cookies

In a medium bowl, combine ice cream and peanuts, chocolate chips or marshmallows (or a combination of these ingredients can be used). Place in freezer for 20 to 30 minutes. Quickly spoon about 2 tablespoons of the ice cream mixture over the flat side of 15 cookies; top with remaining cookies to form sandwiches. Wrap sandwiches individually in plastic wrap. Freeze for 1 to 2 hours or until firm.

Berry Peachy Frozen Dessert

Makes 9 servings

1 (8 oz.) pkg. fat-free
cream cheese, softened

2 (6 oz.) cartons peach
yogurt

½ (8 oz.) tub whipped
topping

1 C. peeled and chopped
fresh peaches

1 C. fresh blueberries

In a medium mixing bowl, beat together cream cheese and yogurt at medium speed until smooth. Fold in whipped topping, peaches and blueberries. Transfer mixture to a 9″ square baking dish; cover and freeze for 8 hours or until firm. Let stand at room temperature for about 30 minutes before cutting into squares and serving.

BOMBS AWAY!

On hot summer days, take your mind off the heat by having a water gun fight. Equip each player with plenty of artillery (including water balloon grenades) and arrange an outdoor water filling station. The filling station should be a designated "safe zone" where players can fill their guns without the threat of being bombarded by other players. Dress appropriately and be prepared to get soaking wet!

Caramel Pops

Makes 4 servings

1 C. ice cream with chocolate-covered peanuts and small peanut butter-filled chocolate candies, such as Blue Bunny's Bunny Tracks

1 C. popped caramel popcorn

Divide the ice cream into four portions. Using an ice cream scoop, shape each portion into a round ball. Roll each ball in the popcorn until completely coated. Insert a wooden craft stick through the popcorn into the ice cream center. Wrap each treat in plastic wrap and place in the freezer for at least 2 hours.

Tropical Sundaes

Makes 4 servings

½ (12.2 oz.) jar caramel topping

⅓ C. pure maple syrup

2 C. butter brickle or butter pecan ice cream, divided

½ C. sliced fresh mango or papaya, divided

½ C. fresh or canned pineapple chunks, drained, divided

4 T. shredded coconut, toasted*, divided

In a small bowl, combine caramel topping and syrup; mix well and set aside. Fill each of four sundae glasses with ¼ cup of ice cream. Top each portion with some of the caramel mixture, some of the mango and a few pineapple chunks. Fill each glass with another ¼ cup of ice cream. Top with the remaining mango and pineapple. Drizzle the remaining caramel sauce and 1 tablespoon of the toasted coconut over each sundae. Serve immediately.

See page 17 for toasting instructions

Cherry Pie Parfaits

Makes 4 servings

3 C. vanilla ice cream

2 (4.5 oz.) pkgs. cherry snack pie

Pecan halves for garnish

Layer about ½ cup of ice cream into each of four parfait glasses. Break the cherry snack pies into pieces; sprinkle over the ice cream in each glass. Top off each glass with another ¼ cup of ice cream. Garnish the parfaits with a few pecan halves. Serve immediately. For a variation, apple or lemon snack pies can be used in place of the cherry snack pie.

White Chocolate Berry Sundaes

Makes 4 servings

½ C. fresh raspberries or strawberries

1 T. sugar

2 C. raspberry sherbet or strawberry ice cream

White chocolate shavings

In a small bowl, combine the berries and sugar; mix lightly and slightly mash some of the berries. Let the berries stand at room temperature until slightly syrupy. Fill each of four sundae glasses with ¼ cup of sherbet or ice cream. Top each portion with some of the berries and syrup. Fill each glass with another ¼ cup of sherbet or ice cream. Top with the remaining berries and syrup. Garnish each sundae with a few white chocolate shavings. Serve immediately.

Easy Chocolate Peanut Butter Pie

Makes 1 (9″) pie

2 (4 oz.) pkgs. single-serving chocolate pudding cups

⅓ C. creamy peanut butter

1 (8 oz.) tub whipped topping

1 (9″) prepared graham cracker pie crust

In a large bowl, combine pudding and peanut butter; stir until smooth. Fold in whipped topping. Pour filling into prepared crust. Cover and freeze until firm. Let stand at room temperature for about 1 hour before cutting into slices and serving.

I SCREAM, YOU SCREAM

July 7th is National Strawberry Sundae Day! Throw a party to celebrate this special holiday. Set out several types of ice cream and various toppings so each guest can create their own special sundae. Have fun dreaming about the various ice cream flavors you would invent if you worked at an ice cream factory.

Peanut Buster Parfait Dessert

Makes 10 to 12 servings

1 lb. chocolate sandwich cookies, crushed

1 C. butter or margarine, melted, divided

1¾ C. powdered sugar

1 (12 oz.) can evaporated milk

1 C. chocolate chips

1 tsp. vanilla extract

½ gallon vanilla ice cream, softened

1½ C. dry roasted peanuts

Combine crushed cookies and ½ cup melted butter; press into bottom of 9 x 13″ baking dish. Chill crust in refrigerator for 1 hour. In a medium saucepan over medium heat, combine powdered sugar, evaporated milk, chocolate chips and remaining ½ cup melted butter; bring to a boil for 8 minutes, stirring constantly. Remove from heat and stir in vanilla; cool. Spread ice cream over the crust. Sprinkle peanuts over ice cream. Pour cooled chocolate sauce over peanuts. Cover and freeze for 8 hours or overnight. Let stand at room temperature for 30 minutes before cutting into squares and serving.

Lemon Ice Dessert

Makes 6 servings

1 C. heavy whipping cream, chilled

½ C. sugar

¼ C. white wine

2 T. lemon juice

1 tsp. grated lemon zest

¼ tsp. ground nutmeg

Fresh mint leaves

In a chilled bowl, whisk together heavy cream and sugar until cream begins to thicken. Gradually whip in white wine, lemon juice and lemon zest. Continue to whip until mixture is light and fluffy, but not grainy. Cover and chill in the refrigerator. Spoon mixture into parfait glasses and garnish each serving with a dash of nutmeg and sprig of fresh mint.

Frangelico Hazelnut Bombe

Makes 8 to 10 servings

3 C. raspberry or orange sorbet or sherbet, softened

1½ C. heavy cream

½ C. honey

¼ C. Frangelico liqueur

1 T. grated orange zest

½ C. hazelnuts, coarsely chopped

Chill a 6-cup stainless steel bowl in the freezer. Evenly pack the sorbet into the bottom and up the sides of the chilled bowl; return to freezer. In a medium mixing bowl, beat together cream, honey and Frangelico until soft peaks form; fold in orange zest and hazelnuts. Spoon filling into sorbet-lined bowl. Level the surface of the filling, cover with plastic wrap and freeze for 8 hours or overnight. To serve, dip the top of the bowl in hot water for 20 to 30 seconds. Invert the bombe onto a serving plate. Cut into wedges and serve immediately.

Slushies, Smoothies & Coolers

Tangy Lemonade Twister

Makes 8 servings

2 C. lemonade

2 C. orange juice

1 liter cold ginger ale

Ice cubes

In a large pitcher, combine lemonade and orange juice; mix well and refrigerate until ready to serve. Divide mixture evenly into eight tall glasses. Fill each glass with ginger ale and add a few ice cubes.

Orange Energy Sports Drink

Makes 4 cups

2 C. water

¼ C. sugar

¼ tsp. salt

¼ C. orange juice

1¾ C. caffeine-free herbal tea

In a large microwave-safe measuring cup, combine water, sugar and salt; heat in microwave until sugar and salt are dissolved, about 1 minute. Let liquid cool to a warm temperature. Stir in orange juice and tea. Chill in refrigerator until ready to serve.

Hawaiian Iced Tea

Makes 8 servings

4 C. simmering hot water   Ice cubes

4 orange pekoe tea bags   Fresh pineapple spears

4 C. ice cold water

1 (16 oz.) can pineapple
  juice

Carefully pour the simmering water into a large pitcher; add the tea bags and steep for about 4 minutes. Remove the tea bags and add the cold water to the pitcher. Stir in the pineapple juice. Refrigerate until thoroughly chilled. Fill eight tall glasses with ice. Pour the tea over the ice. Garnish each serving with a spear of fresh pineapple.

THINK OUTSIDE THE POOL
If your local swimming pool is too packed on the hottest of days, take advantage of air-conditioned places. Stroll through an enclosed mall or catch a flick at the always-cool movie theater. Spend a day reading at the city library or check out the exhibits at a local museum.

Brazilian Limeade

Makes 4 servings

2 limes

½ C. sugar

3 T. sweetened condensed
  milk

3 C. water

Ice cubes, divided

Wash limes thoroughly and cut off the ends. Slice each lime into eight wedges. Place the wedges, including the peel, in a blender. Add sugar, sweetened condensed milk, water and 10 ice cubes. Pulse until well blended. Strain the liquid into a pitcher through a fine mesh strainer to remove any rinds and large ice pieces. Fill four tall glasses with ice. Pour the limeade over the ice.

Apple Juleps

Makes 6 servings

4 C. apple juice

1 C. orange juice

1 C. pineapple juice

¼ C. lemon juice

Ice cubes

Fresh mint leaves

In a large pitcher, combine the apple juice, orange juice, pineapple juice and lemon juice. Mix until all juices are well combined. Fill six tall glasses with ice and a few mint leaves. Pour the juice over the ice.

PAINLESS PICNICKING

Warm summer months are the perfect time to go on a picnic. But a picnic can quickly turn into a frenzied pack-unpack-repack feast instead of the carefree open-air meal it was intended to be. For an untroubled afternoon, simply pack grab-and-go items such as bottled drinks, fruit, a small loaf of French bread or crackers, and a few wedges of spreadable cheese. Just throw in a blanket and off you go!

Pink Passion Lemonade

Makes 2 quarts

8 C. water, divided

3 fresh strawberries, sliced

1 C. sugar

½ C. brown sugar

1 tsp. honey

1¾ C. lemon juice

1 orange, sliced

In a large saucepan, combine 1 cup water, strawberries, sugar, brown sugar and honey. Bring mixture to a boil, reduce heat and simmer for 10 minutes, stirring occasionally. Remove from stovetop and cool to room temperature; cover and chill in refrigerator. In a large pitcher, combine remaining 7 cups water, lemon juice and orange slices. Stir in cooled syrup. Chill until ready to serve.

Strawberry Banana Smoothie

Makes 1 serving

1 ripe banana, peeled

¼ C. sliced fresh
   strawberries

⅓ C. skim or 1% milk

1 (6 oz.) carton low-fat
   plain or vanilla yogurt

In a blender, combine banana, strawberries, milk and yogurt. Blend until smooth. Pour into a tall, chilled glass.

BERRY FRESH

You can't get much fresher than berries off the vine. Contact a local berry farm to ask if they allow patrons to pick their own berries for a fee. While you're there, ask about additional fruit seasons. They might also harvest apples, peaches, pumpkins or other fruits and vegetables later in the year.

Blueberry Smoothie

Makes 1 serving

1 C. skim or 1% milk
¾ C. fresh blueberries
1 T. sugar

½ tsp. vanilla extract
3 ice cubes

In a blender, combine milk, blueberries, sugar, vanilla and ice cubes. Blend until ice is chopped and ingredients are frothy. Pour into a tall, chilled glass.

Orange Strawberry Smoothie

Makes 1 serving

1 small orange, peeled and pith removed
4 large fresh strawberries, halved
¾ C. unflavored liquid creamer

1 tsp. vanilla extract
1 tsp. sugar
6 ice cubes

Divide the orange into segments. In a blender, combine orange segments, strawberries, creamer, vanilla, sugar and ice cubes. Blend until ice is chopped and ingredients are frothy. Pour into a tall, chilled glass.

PUPPY LOVE

Beating the heat is extra tough on the dog days of summer, but it's even harder for man's best friend. The only ways dogs can cool themselves is by panting and sweating through their paw pads. Keep your dog well-hydrated and cool. Only go for walks in the early morning or after the sun has set. And remember: never leave a dog in a parked car. Even on a mild 73°F day, the temperature inside a car can reach 120°F in 30 minutes. On a 90°F day, the interior of a vehicle can reach 160°F in just a short amount of time.

Peachy Yogurt Smoothie

Makes 4 servings

1 (6 oz.) carton low-fat peach yogurt

2½ C. whipped topping

2 C. sliced fresh peaches

2 C. ice cubes

In a blender, combine yogurt, whipped topping, peaches and ice. Blend until ice is chopped and ingredients are frothy. Pour into a tall, chilled glass.

Smart Start Smoothie

Makes 1 serving

4 long carrots, peeled
½ C. orange juice
2 strawberry cream
  frozen juice bars

1 (6 oz.) carton low-fat
  plain yogurt
½ banana, peeled

If you have a juicer, extract juice from carrots and pour into blender with orange juice. If you do not have a juicer, use only 2 carrots. Add peeled carrots to blender with orange juice. Unwrap juice bars and remove the sticks. Add juice bars, yogurt and banana to blender. Blend until smooth. Pour into a tall, chilled glass.

Citrus Frosty

Makes 4 servings

3 C. orange sherbet
1 (6 oz.) can frozen
  orange juice concentrate
1 (6 oz.) carton lemon
  yogurt

2 T. lemon juice
1½ tsp. vanilla extract

In a blender, combine sherbet, orange juice concentrate, yogurt, lemon juice and vanilla. Blend until smooth. Pour into four short, chilled glasses.

Pineapple Coolers

Makes 4 servings

½ fresh pineapple,
  peeled, cored and cut
  into chunks

2 C. pineapple juice
¼ tsp. coconut extract
10 ice cubes

In a blender, combine pineapple chunks, pineapple juice and coconut extract; pulse until well blended. Add a few ice cubes at a time, blending after each addition until ice is chopped. Pour into four short, chilled glasses.

WORKIN' AT THE CAR WASH

Cold weather can take its toll on your vehicle. But when summer comes around, it is time to scrub off winter's grit and grime. Washing your car at home costs less than taking it to the drive-through or coin washers, and it can be a great way to cool off and get some exercise. Remember to use a soap made especially for washing cars, since many household detergents are too harsh and can damage the paint. In addition, use a washing mitt made for cars rather than a sea sponge, which could contain traces of sand.

Sweet Nectar Cooler

Makes 8 servings

1 (12 oz.) can frozen
  limeade concentrate

2½ C. lemon-lime soda

2½ C. grapefruit soda

2½ T. honey

Green food coloring,
  optional

Ice cubes

In a tall pitcher, combine limeade concentrate, lemon-lime soda, grapefruit soda and honey; mix until limeade concentrate is completely dissolved. If desired, stir in drops of green food coloring until mixture is a light green color. Refrigerate until ready to serve. Pour into tall glasses over ice.

Peach Cooler

Makes 2 servings

1 (12 oz.) can lemon-
  lime soda

1 fresh peach, peeled and
  halved, or 2 canned
  peach halves, drained

1 tsp. lemon juice

2 scoops vanilla ice
  cream, divided

¼ C. crushed ice, divided

In a blender, combine soda, peach halves and lemon juice; blend until smooth. Pour into two tall, chilled glasses. Top each serving with a scoop of vanilla ice cream and crushed ice.

Sangria Slushies

Makes 4 servings

1 orange, peeled and pith removed

1 lime, peeled and seeded

½ C. grape juice

1 C. orange juice

1 C. fresh or canned pineapple chunks, drained

1 tsp. vanilla extract

2 T. brandy or 1 tsp. brandy extract

1 (12 oz.) can lemon-lime soda

4 raspberry frozen juice bars

Divide the orange into segments. In a blender, combine orange segments, lime flesh, grape juice, orange juice, pineapple chunks, vanilla, brandy and soda; blend until smooth. Unwrap juice bars and remove the sticks. Add juice bars and blend until smooth. Pour into four chilled wine glasses or champagne flutes.

Honey Hurricane

Makes 2 servings

2 C. vanilla ice cream

1 T. honey

¼ C. shredded coconut

½ C. chopped almonds

1 oz. vodka

1 oz. light rum

¼ C. whipped topping, divided

In a blender, combine ice cream, honey, coconut, almonds, vodka and rum; blend until smooth. Pour into two tall, chilled glasses. Add a dollop of whipped topping to the top of each serving.

MELON MANIA

*For a fun adult treat, try making
a vodka watermelon. You will need a miniature
(not seedless) watermelon and 375-milliliter
bottle of vodka. Cut a small circle through
the skin and rind of the watermelon,
exposing the fruit inside. Open the bottle
of vodka and insert the open end of the bottle
into the watermelon with good force. Set aside
for 1 to 2 hours, allowing the vodka
to flow into and disperse through the fruit.
Remove the bottle and carefully
transfer the watermelon to the
freezer for 1 to 2 hours.
Cut the watermelon into
slices and enjoy!*

Coffee Smoothie

Makes 1 serving

1 C. skim or 1% milk   2 T. chocolate syrup
1 T. instant coffee   7 ice cubes
2 T. sugar

In a blender, combine milk, instant coffee, sugar,
chocolate syrup and ice cubes. Blend until smooth
and frothy. Pour into a tall, chilled drink glass.

Mocha Mudslide

Makes 1 serving

1 C. chocolate milk   ½ tsp. vanilla extract
½ C. vanilla ice cream

In a blender, combine chocolate milk, ice cream and vanilla; blend until smooth. Pour into a tall, chilled drink glass.

KALEIDOSCOPE COOLER

For a flavorful rainbow slushie, freeze assorted fruit juices separately in paper cups. Once frozen, peel away the cups and place each frozen juice in a separate heavy-duty freezer bag. Close the bags and crush the juice into icy crystals with the side of a hammer or wooden mallet. Layer the various types of crushed frozen juices into tall clear glasses or dessert cups; eat with a spoon.

Watermelon Slushies

Makes 4 servings

2 C. seeded watermelon chunks

2 C. halved fresh strawberries

⅓ C. sugar

⅓ C. lemon juice

2 C. crushed ice

In a blender, combine watermelon chunks, strawberries, sugar and lemon juice; blend until smooth. Pour mixture into ice cube trays; freeze until solid. Remove from freezer and set at room temperature for 15 minutes. Blend fruit cubes in blender with crushed ice until slushy. Pour into short, chilled glasses.

Rum Slushies

Makes 24 servings

2½ C. light or dark rum

1 (46 oz.) can pineapple juice

1 (16 oz.) jar maraschino cherries in syrup

1 (6 oz.) can frozen lemonade concentrate

1 C. water

1 liter lemon-lime soda

In a large pitcher or bowl, combine rum, pineapple juice, cherries with syrup, lemonade concentrate, water and lemon-lime soda; mix until well combined. Pour or scoop liquid into several ice cube trays or plastic cups; freeze until solid. Remove from freezer as needed and set at room temperature for 15 minutes. Blend rum-fruit cubes in blender until slushy. Pour into short, chilled glasses.

Variation: For a less frozen slushy, prepare as above but omit soda from frozen mixture. Freeze and blend as directed; divide into glasses. Pour about 1 cup lemon-lime soda over each serving.

GOING GREEN

Make your neighbors green with envy!
One of the keys to a grassy lawn is picking the
right grass seeds for your climate.
Pay attention to the growing conditions in
your area, such as little rain or lots of sunlight,
and pick a grass that will accommodate your
climate. Over-seed your lawn each fall by
spreading new seeds over the growing grass.
And remember:
a thicker lawn helps crowd out the weeds.

Chocolate Peanut Butter Shakes

Makes 4 servings

1 C. creamy peanut
  butter

¼ C. chocolate syrup

1 C. milk

12 ice cubes

In a blender, combine peanut butter, chocolate syrup, milk and ice cubes; blend until smooth and creamy. Pour into four tall, chilled glasses.

Banana Pudding Shake

Makes 2 servings

1½ C. skim or 1% milk
1 medium banana, peeled
½ C. vanilla ice cream or
  frozen yogurt

5 vanilla wafers
1 tsp. vanilla extract

In a blender, combine milk, banana, ice cream, vanilla wafers and vanilla; blend until smooth and creamy. Pour into four tall, chilled glasses.

Aloha Shake

Makes 2 servings

1 C. sliced fresh mango
  or peach
¼ C. pineapple juice

¼ C. sugar
2 C. vanilla ice cream
¾ C. skim or 1% milk

In a blender, combine mango, pineapple juice and sugar; blend until smooth. Add ice cream and milk; pulse until well blended. Pour into two tall, chilled glasses.

Frrrozen Hot Chocolate

Makes 1 serving

3 oz. milk chocolate bar, chopped

2 tsp. hot chocolate mix

1½ T. sugar

1½ C. milk, divided

3 C. ice cubes

Whipped cream

Chocolate shavings

In a double boiler over low heat, melt chocolate bar pieces, stirring occasionally. Add hot chocolate mix and sugar, stirring until completely melted. Remove from heat and slowly stir in ½ cup milk; cool to room temperature. In a blender, combine cooled chocolate mixture, remaining 1 cup milk and ice; blend until smooth. Pour into a tall, chilled glass and top with a dollop of whipped cream and chocolate shavings.

BE A CONSCIOUS CRUISER

If boating is in your summer plans, you can help prevent the amount of pollution expelled in the air and water by adopting these practices: limit the amount of engine operation at full throttle, eliminate unnecessary idling, pour gasoline slowly to avoid spills, and always pack plenty of bags to remove your garbage and any polluted items you care to pick up while out on the water.

Orange Sherbet Punch

Makes 24 servings

1 qt. vanilla ice cream
1 qt. orange sherbet
1 (16 oz.) bottle lemon-
  lime soda

4 C. 1% or 2% milk

Cut vanilla ice cream and orange sherbet into pieces; place in the bottom of a large punch bowl. Pour soda and milk over ice cream and sherbet. Stir gently and serve immediately.

Wine Cooler Punch

Makes 24 servings

3 (6 oz.) cans frozen pink
  lemonade concentrate,
  divided
1 (6 oz.) can water
1 (10 oz.) jar maraschino
  cherries, drained
1 (2 liter) bottle lemon-
  lime soda

1 (750 ml.) bottle
  red wine
1 orange, sliced
1 lemon, sliced

In a pitcher, combine 1 can of lemonade concentrate with 1 can of water; mix until well blended. Pour mixture into ice cubes trays. Place 1 cherry in each cube; freeze until solid. In a large punch bowl, combine remaining 2 cans of lemonade concentrate, lemon-lime soda and wine; mix until well blended. Float cherry ice cubes in punch and garnish with orange and lemon slices.

PICTURE PERFECT

To make the most of your summer photographs, try to snap outdoor photos in the "golden hours" right after sunrise and right before sunset. And don't leave the camera behind on overcast days – they are ideal for capturing the best light. Another tip: always make sure the sun is to the photographer's, not the subject's, back.

Sweet Tea Punch

Makes 24 servings

3 C. water

5 tea bags

1½ C. sugar

1½ C. orange juice

1½ C. unsweetened
 pineapple juice

½ C. lemon juice

4 C. ginger ale

Fresh mint leaves

Bring water to a boil in a large saucepan over medium-high heat. Remove from the heat and add tea bags; steep for 5 minutes. Remove tea bags from saucepan and add sugar, stirring until sugar is completely dissolved; chill in refrigerator for 3 hours. Pour chilled tea into a large punch bowl. Add orange juice, pineapple juice and lemon juice; mix well. Just before serving, stir in ginger ale. Garnish each punch glass with a few mint leaves. Ladle punch into glasses over leaves.

Summer Snacks

Margarita Dip

Makes about 1½ cups

1 (8 oz.) pkg. cream
cheese, softened

⅓ C. frozen margarita
drink mix, thawed

2 T. orange juice

¼ C. powdered sugar

¼ C. whipped topping

In a medium mixing bowl, beat together cream
cheese, margarita drink mix, orange juice and
powdered sugar at medium speed until smooth.
Fold in whipped topping until well blended.
Cover and chill in refrigerator for at least 1 hour.
Serve dip with strawberries, cherries, peach slices,
graham crackers or shortbread cookies.

Strawberry Salsa

Makes about 1½ cups

1 (10 to 12 count) box
chunky strawberry
frozen juice bars

¾ C. chopped red onion

2 jalapeno peppers,
seeded and chopped

¼ C. chopped fresh
cilantro

2 tsp. lime juice

2 tsp. pineapple juice

Pinch of salt and pepper

Unwrap juice bars and remove the sticks. Melt the
juice bars in a large saucepan over low heat; simmer
until liquid is reduced by half. Transfer liquid to a
plastic bowl; refrigerate until cool. Once cool, stir in
onion, jalapeno, cilantro, lime juice and pineapple
juice. Season to taste with salt and pepper. Serve
salsa with tortilla chips.

Cucumber Salsa

Makes 3 cups

2 cucumbers, peeled, seeded and chopped

1 C. sour cream

1 C. plain yogurt

¼ C. chopped fresh parsley

¼ C. chopped fresh cilantro

1 tsp. ground cumin

½ tsp. salt

In a medium bowl, combine cucumber, sour cream, yogurt, parsley, cilantro, cumin and salt; mix well. Cover bowl and refrigerate salsa for at least 2 hours. Serve dip with cut vegetables, chips, crackers or rye bread squares.

STAR LIGHT, STAR BRIGHT

Each summer there is at least one warm night where the sky is so clear and bright that you feel like you could touch the stars. Be prepared for this night by researching the summer constellations visible from earth. Download and print one of the many summer star charts available on the internet, or check out a book about constellations from your local library.

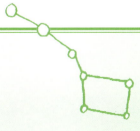

Black Bean and Grilled Corn Salsa

Makes 5 cups

1 jalapeno pepper

1 red bell pepper

4 ears fresh corn, shucked

¼ C. lime juice

1 (15 oz.) can black beans, drained and rinsed

½ C. coarsely chopped fresh parsley

¼ C. finely chopped red onion

½ tsp. minced garlic

1 T. extra-virgin olive oil

¼ tsp. cayenne pepper

½ tsp. salt

¼ tsp. pepper

Heat an outdoor grill to medium-high heat. Place jalapeno and red bell pepper on the grill; cook, turning occasionally, until the peppers' skin is black all over, about 5 to 10 minutes for the jalapeno and 10 to 15 minutes for the red pepper. Place grilled peppers in a brown paper bag; fold over bag to close. After 10 minutes, peel away and discard black skin (do not rinse peppers). Remove and discard stems and seeds from peppers. Mince jalapeno and cut red pepper into ¼" pieces; set aside. Place ears of corn directly on grill; heat until brown and tender, turning often. After about 10 minutes remove corn from grill and let cool slightly. Cut kernels from the cob with a sharp knife. In a medium bowl, combine peppers, corn, lime juice, black beans, parsley, red onion and garlic. Mix in olive oil and cayenne pepper. Season to taste with salt and pepper. Serve salsa with tortilla chips.

Cold Crab Dip

Makes about 2½ cups

2 (8 oz.) pkgs. cream cheese, softened

3 T. milk

2 green onions, finely chopped

2 T. prepared horseradish

2 (6 oz.) cans crabmeat, drained, picked over and flaked

In a medium bowl, combine cream cheese, milk, green onions and horseradish. Mix well, then gradually stir in crabmeat. Chill dip in refrigerator until ready to serve. Serve dip with assorted crackers and cut vegetables.

Pesto Spinach Spread

Makes about 1 cup

1 (9 oz.) pkg. frozen chopped spinach, thawed

1 C. grated Parmesan cheese

¼ C. fresh basil

2 cloves garlic

¾ C. extra-virgin olive oil

2 T. lemon juice

Drain thawed spinach well by pressing into a strainer until only a little liquid will squeeze out. In a blender or food processor, combine spinach, Parmesan cheese, basil and garlic cloves; process until well blended. While machine is still running, slowly pour in olive oil until mixture is the consistency of thick paste. Turn off machine and stir in lemon juice; cover and refrigerate until ready to serve. Serve spread with cut vegetables and French bread cubes, or spread over bread and pitas to make sandwiches.

SOW WHAT YOU GROW

Take full advantage of summer's natural flavors by planting your own basil. Use seeds, since cuttings don't survive easily. Plant seeds ⅛″ deep after the last frost in spring. If planting outdoors, space the seeds 1′ apart and space rows 2′ apart. Pinch the stems frequently to allow basil to grow bushy and full. Harvest the leaves when young, and prune the main stem before each plant flowers by pinching away all but one node with at least two shoots of leaves. To store basil, dry the leaves or brush them with oil and freeze in freezer-safe bags.

Fruit Ginger Dip

Makes about 2½ cups

1 (3.4 oz.) box instant vanilla pudding mix

1½ C. whole milk

1 (6 oz.) can frozen orange juice concentrate, thawed

⅓ C. sour cream

¼ tsp. ground ginger

1 T. finely chopped candied ginger

½ C. heavy whipping cream

2 T. powdered sugar

In a small bowl, whisk together pudding mix, milk and orange juice concentrate for 1 minute. Stir in sour cream, ground ginger and candied ginger. In a separate mixing bowl, beat heavy cream and powdered sugar until stiff peaks form; fold in ginger mixture. Transfer to a serving bowl and chill at least 2 hours before serving. Serve dip with strawberries, mandarin orange segments, pear slices, grapes and other fruits.

Garden Fresh Salsa

Makes about 4½ cups

½ C. chopped green onions

⅓ C. chopped fresh basil

1 (15 oz.) can whole kernel corn, drained

1 (15 oz.) can black beans, drained and rinsed

1 medium green bell pepper, seeded and chopped

2 large tomatoes, diced

2 tsp. minced garlic

3 T. lime juice

3 T. red wine vinegar

2 T. extra-virgin olive oil

1 tsp. salt

In a large bowl, combine green onions, basil, corn, black beans, bell pepper and tomatoes; set aside. In a medium bowl, whisk together garlic, lime juice, vinegar, olive oil and salt. Pour liquid over vegetables and toss until well combined. Transfer to a serving bowl and chill at least 2 hours before serving. Serve salsa with tortilla chips.

BURNING WITH STYLE

A fireplace doesn't have to be reserved for cold, winter evenings. If you have a fireplace, give it a summer makeover by cleaning out any soot and burnt ash. Place a large decorative urn filled with wildflowers or a flowering plant in the firebox. This will brighten the area, giving it a summery feel.

Strawberry Poppers

Makes 32 servings

32 large fresh strawberries

1 (12 oz.) tub cream cheese, softened

½ C. powdered sugar

¼ tsp. almond extract

2 (1 oz.) squares milk chocolate, grated

Cut a thin slice from the stem end of each strawberry, allowing each berry to stand upright on the flat end. Carefully cut each berry into four wedges, being careful not to cut entirely through the berries. Fan out the four wedges slightly, being careful not to break the berries apart; set aside. In a small mixing bowl, beat together cream cheese, powdered sugar and almond extract until light and fluffy. Gently fold in grated chocolate. Using a teaspoon or a decorating bag with a tip, carefully fill each strawberry with a portion of the filling. If desired, sprinkle a little more grated chocolate over the berries; refrigerate until ready to serve.

Italian Stuffed Cherry Tomatoes

Makes 36 servings

36 cherry tomatoes
1 (8 oz.) pkg. cream cheese, softened
1 T. dry Italian salad dressing mix

2 T. milk
3 T. chopped fresh parsley

Place tomatoes, stem-side down, on a cutting board. Using a sharp knife, cut an "X" in each tomato to within ¼" of the bottom end, being careful not to cut entirely through the tomatoes. Gently fan out the tomatoes slightly, being careful not to break the tomatoes apart; set aside. In a small bowl, combine cream cheese, Italian dressing mix and milk, mixing until well blended and smooth. Fill each tomato with about 1 teaspoon of the cream cheese mixture. Sprinkle tops of tomatoes with parsley. Serve immediately or chill in refrigerator until ready to serve.

Avocado Carrot Salad

Makes 1½ cups

1 large ripe avocado, peeled, seeded and diced
¼ C. shredded carrots

1 T. Italian salad dressing
½ tsp. salt

In a medium bowl, combine avocado, carrots, salad dressing and salt. Mix until all ingredients are well blended. Serve as a summer side dish or as a dip for tortilla chips and crackers.

Mini Chicken Pizzas

Makes 12 mini pizzas

1 C. creamy Alfredo sauce, divided

6 English muffins, split

1 T. chopped fresh basil, divided

1 (4 oz.) can sliced olives, drained, divided

4 green onions, thinly sliced, divided

1 small tomato, diced, divided

1 (9 oz.) can chunk chicken, drained, divided

1½ C. shredded mozzarella cheese, divided

Preheat oven broiler or set toaster oven to high setting. Spread some of the Alfredo sauce over each muffin half; sprinkle with some basil. Top each with some olives, green onions, tomato and chicken. Sprinkle cheese over toppings on each muffin. Toast in oven, a few at a time, until toppings are hot and cheese is melted. If using an oven broiler, place pizzas on a baking sheet lined with nonstick foil; broil until cheese is melted.

Cucumber Tuna Snack Sandwiches

Makes 8 mini sandwiches

4 English muffins, split

1 (6 oz.) can tuna, drained

2 T. mayonnaise

2 T. finely chopped celery

Dash of Worcestershire sauce

2 tsp. chili sauce

1 T. lemon juice

1 small cucumber, sliced, divided

Toast muffin halves until lightly browned. Combine tuna, mayonnaise, celery, Worcestershire sauce, chili sauce and lemon juice; mix well, adding more mayonnaise as desired. Spread mixture over each toasted muffin. Top with slices of cucumber. Serve as open-face sandwiches.

Veggie Deli Snack Wraps

Makes 8 mini wraps

2 to 3 T. garden vegetable cream cheese, softened, divided

2 (10") flour or spinach tortillas

¼ C. shredded carrots, divided

¼ C. shredded Cheddar cheese, divided

½ C. shredded lettuce, divided

2 T. sliced black olives, optional, divided

4 slices deli ham or turkey, divided

Spread 1 to 1½ tablespoons of the cream cheese over each tortilla, spreading all the way to the edge of each tortilla. Press 2 tablespoons of the shredded carrots and shredded cheese over the cream cheese on each tortilla. Spread the shredded lettuce and black olives over the carrots and cheese. Layer 2 slices of deli meat over the ingredients on each tortilla. Roll up the tortillas. Cut each tortilla into 4 even pieces, securing each piece with a toothpick. Serve immediately.

BUG SPRAY BASICS

It wouldn't be summer without the familiar smell of insect repellent. But even a product as helpful as bug spray has some limitations. Since heavy saturation is unnecessary, apply repellent sparingly and only on exposed skin surfaces or on top of clothing. Spray only in well-ventilated areas and avoid breathing in the mists or spraying near food. Never apply repellent to open wounds or irritated skin. Take care when applying repellent to the neck and face, avoiding the eye area. If you get repellent in your eyes, rinse them immediately with water.

Turkey Avocado Rounds

Makes 8 mini sandwiches

4 English muffins, split

2 T. butter, divided

8 slices deli turkey, divided

8 strips bacon, cooked crisp, divided

1 avocado, peeled, seeded and sliced, divided

8 slices Swiss cheese, divided

Alfalfa sprouts, divided, optional

Toast muffin halves until lightly browned. Spread some butter over each toasted muffin. Place one turkey slice on each. Break each piece of bacon in half; place two halves over the turkey on each muffin. Top each with a few avocado slices and one cheese slice. Microwave sandwiches, a few at a time, until the cheese is melted. Top with alfalfa sprouts, if desired. Serve as open-face sandwiches.

Picnic Baguette Snackers

Makes 8 to 12 servings

½ (8 oz.) tub cream cheese with chives and onion

1 T. lemon juice

1 T. Dijon mustard

1 (8 oz.) French baguette, split

8 oz. deli smoked turkey slices

4 slices provolone or Swiss cheese

1 (7 oz.) jar roasted sweet peppers, drained and sliced

1 C. baby spinach leaves

Combine cream cheese, lemon juice and mustard; mix well. Spread mixture over both cut sides of baguette. Layer turkey slices, cheese, peppers and spinach over the bottom half of loaf; cover with top half. Slice crosswise into 2″ pieces. Wrap each snack sandwich tightly in plastic wrap; refrigerate until ready to serve.

PERSONAL PEPPERS

For a fun summer party snack, make edible veggie bowls. Cut clean green, yellow and red peppers in half horizontally. Remove any membrane and seeds from the peppers to make personal bowls. Fill each pepper bowl with ranch dressing or vegetable dip. Serve with carrot sticks, celery sticks, pepper slices and cherry tomatoes for dipping.

Broiled Tomato Sandwiches

Makes 4 mini sandwiches

2 T. extra-virgin olive oil

2 T. balsamic vinegar

1 large tomato, cut into thick slices

3 T. mayonnaise

½ tsp. dried parsley

¼ tsp. dried oregano

¼ tsp. pepper

3 T. grated Parmesan cheese, divided

4 slices white or wheat bread, toasted

Preheat oven broiler or set toaster oven to high setting. In a medium bowl, whisk together olive oil and vinegar. Add tomato slices to bowl, allowing tomatoes to marinate, stirring occasionally. Meanwhile, combine mayonnaise, parsley, oregano, pepper and 4 teaspoons Parmesan cheese; mix well and spread over toasted bread. Place a few marinated tomato slices on each piece of toast; sprinkle with remaining Parmesan cheese. Toast in oven, a few at a time, until toppings are hot and cheese is melted. If using an oven broiler, place sandwiches on a baking sheet lined with nonstick foil; broil until cheese is melted.

Microwave Popcorn Balls

Makes 5 to 8 popcorn balls

5 C. popped popcorn

½ C. miniature chocolate chips, toffee chips or M&Ms

⅓ C. chopped peanuts

2 T. butter or margarine, softened

3 C. miniature marshmallows

In a large bowl, combine popcorn, chocolate chips and peanuts; toss until evenly mixed. Place butter and marshmallows in a large microwaveable bowl; microwave on high for 2 minutes, until melted and smooth, stirring after 1 minute. Quickly pour marshmallow mixture over popcorn and stir until evenly coated. With buttered hands, quickly shape mixture into balls; place on waxed paper until cooled, about 1 hour.

Chocolate Fruit Cones

Makes 4 servings

⅓ C. semi-sweet chocolate chips

1 tsp. shortening

4 flat-bottom ice cream cones

Candy sprinkles

3 C. chopped fresh fruit, divided

4 tsp. honey, divided

4 tsp. granola or chopped peanuts, divided

In a microwaveable glass dish, combine chocolate chips and shortening; microwave for 1 minute, stirring until melted. If necessary, return to microwave for 15 second intervals until completely melted. Dip the rim end of each cone in the melted chocolate. Roll the edge in sprinkles; set aside to dry. Divide the fruit evenly into each cone. Drizzle 1 teaspoon honey over the fruit and top with 1 teaspoon granola or peanuts.

Peanut Butter Banana Wraps

Makes 4 servings

½ C. creamy peanut butter, divided

4 (8 to 10") whole wheat or flour tortillas

¼ C. honey

2 small bananas, peeled and sliced

¼ C. miniature semi-sweet chocolate chips

Spread 2 tablespoons peanut butter over each tortilla. Drizzle 1 tablespoon honey over the peanut butter on each tortilla; top each with some of the banana slices and chocolate chips. Roll up each tortilla and serve immediately.

WHEN IT RAINS, IT POURS

Warm rising air combined with moisture and a light breeze makes the perfect recipe for a summer thunderstorm. More than 40,000 thunderstorms occur all over the world each day, and most last for only half an hour. The lightning and thunder show produced by a storm can be spectacular, but it can also be dangerous. While inside during a storm, stay off landline phones and away from windows. Avoid taking a shower or bath, and have flashlights handy in case the power goes out. If you're caught driving in a thunderstorm, reduce your speed or pull off the road if necessary. Turn on your emergency flashers and remain in your vehicle until the storm passes. If you're outdoors during a storm, crouch low away from trees, tall objects and water. Try to find shelter in a building. Boaters and swimmers should get to land as soon as possible.

Honey Crisp Cookies

Makes about 30 cookies

½ C. powdered sugar	1½ C. crispy rice cereal
½ C. honey	½ C. raisins
½ C. peanut butter	½ C. candy sprinkles

Cover a baking sheet with waxed paper. In a medium bowl, combine powdered sugar, honey and peanut butter, mixing well. Stir in cereal and raisins. Quickly shape the mixture into 1″ balls by hand. Roll each ball in the sprinkles; place on baking sheet. Chill in the refrigerator for 1 hour. Store cookies in an air-tight container in the refrigerator.

Mallow Snack Squares

Makes 8 servings

1½ C. flaky corn cereal	3 C. miniature marshmallows
1 C. quick or old-fashioned oats	½ C. creamy or chunky peanut butter
½ C. raisins	¼ C. butter or margarine

In a large bowl, combine cereal, oats and raisins; toss until well combined. In a medium saucepan over low heat, combine marshmallows, peanut butter and margarine until melted and smooth. Pour melted mixture over dry ingredients; stir quickly until well combined and press into a lightly greased 8″ square pan. Let cool to room temperature before cutting into small squares.

IF YOU CAN'T STAND THE HEAT...

One of the best ways to keep unwanted heat out of your home during hot summer days is to keep oven use to a minimum. Whenever possible, try to use convenience appliances, such as a microwave, toaster oven, mini grill, rotating pizza oven or counter-top griddle. And, to satisfy your sweet tooth, prepare no-bake treats, such as the recipes below and on surrounding pages.

Just OK   05-24-11

S'mores Squares

Makes 1 dozen

1 (12 oz.) pkg. Golden Grahams cereal

3 C. miniature marshmallows

¾ C. light corn syrup

3 T. butter or margarine

1 (11.5 oz.) pkg. milk chocolate chips

1 tsp. vanilla extract

Place cereal and marshmallows in a large bowl. In a medium saucepan over low heat, combine corn syrup, butter, chocolate chips and vanilla, stirring constantly until almost boiling. Pour melted mixture over cereal; stir quickly until well coated and press into a lightly greased 9 x 13" pan. Let cool to room temperature before cutting into 2" squares.

Strawberry Margarita Bars

Makes 1 dozen

1¼ C. crushed pretzels

¼ C. butter, melted

1 (14 oz.) can sweetened condensed milk

1 C. pureed strawberries

½ C. lime juice

1 (8 oz.) tub whipped topping, thawed

Fresh sliced strawberries for garnish

Mix pretzels and melted butter in a 9 x 13″ baking dish; press firmly into bottom of pan and chill in refrigerator. Combine condensed milk, strawberries and lime juice, mixing well; gently fold in whipped topping. Spread mixture over crust layer; freeze for 6 hours or overnight. Let stand at room temperature for 15 minutes before cutting into squares; garnish with strawberry slices.

No-Bake Brownies

Makes 3 dozen

2½ C. finely crushed graham crackers

2 C. miniature marshmallows

1 C. chopped walnuts, optional

1 (6 oz.) pkg. chocolate chips

1 C. evaporated milk

½ C. light corn syrup

¼ tsp. salt

1 T. butter or margarine

1 T. vanilla extract

Combine graham crackers, marshmallows and walnuts; set aside. In a large saucepan over low heat, combine chocolate chips, evaporated milk, corn syrup and salt; heat to a rapid boil for 10 minutes, stirring constantly. Remove from heat; stir in butter and vanilla. Quickly stir chocolate mixture into crumb mixture; spread into an 8″ or 9″ square pan. Chill brownies in refrigerator for 3 hours or until set; cut into squares. Store in an airtight container in the refrigerator.

Fabulous Fruit

Banana Pops

Makes 10 servings

5 bananas, peeled
5 T. brown sugar
1¼ tsp. ground
   cinnamon

5 T. honey
2½ T. granola

Cut each banana in half crosswise, not lengthwise.
Insert a popsicle stick into cut end of each banana
half. In a small bowl, combine the brown sugar and
cinnamon. In a separate small bowl, combine the
honey and granola. Roll each banana half in either
the brown sugar mixture or the honey mixture.
Wrap each popsicle in aluminum foil; freeze until
ready to serve.

Blueberry
Kiwi Cups

Makes 6 servings

2 C. fresh or frozen
   blueberries, thawed,
   divided
⅛ tsp. ground cinnamon

½ C. heavy whipping
   cream
1 T. sugar
4 kiwis, peeled and diced

In a shallow dish, mash 1 cup blueberries; mix
in cinnamon and set aside. In a medium mixing
bowl, beat heavy cream and sugar until stiff peaks
form; fold in mashed blueberries. Layer half of
the whipped mixture into six small glasses. Top
with a layer of blueberries and kiwi, then top with
remaining whipped mixture. Serve immediately or
chill in refrigerator for up to 2 hours.

Sweet Tart Salad

Makes 4 servings

1½ lbs. fresh
strawberries, sliced

2½ T. brown sugar

1 T. balsamic vinegar

¼ tsp. pepper

In a large bowl, toss sliced berries with brown sugar;
let stand at room temperature for 10 minutes. In a
small bowl, combine the vinegar and pepper; pour
over berries and toss until well coated. Divide salad
into four small serving bowls.

EVADE THE FADE

*Chlorine and salt water can do a number
on your swimsuit. Before the first use of
a new swimsuit, wash it in a solution of
1 tablespoon of white vinegar mixed with
1 quart of water for 30 minutes. This will help
slow down the fading process. Immediately
after swimming in chlorinated or salt water,
rinse your suit in cold water.*

Peach-a-Berry Salad

Makes 4 servings

3 whole fresh peaches   ¼ C. honey

5 C. fresh blackberries   ½ tsp. ground cardamom

2 C. sliced fresh strawberries

Fill a medium pot with water and bring to a boil. Add peaches to boiling water for 30 seconds to blanch. Drain pot and transfer peaches to a medium bowl. Cover peaches with cold water to cool. Once cooled, drain, peel and slice the peaches. In a medium bowl, combine peaches, blackberries, strawberries, honey and cardamom; toss until evenly mixed. Divide salad into four small serving bowls.

Grilled Cantaloupe Skewers

Makes 4 servings

1 cantaloupe, peeled,   ½ C. honey
  seeded and cubed   ⅓ C. chopped fresh mint

¼ C. butter

Preheat an outdoor grill to medium heat and lightly oil the grate. Thread the cubed cantaloupe onto four long skewers. In a small saucepan over low heat, melt butter and honey; stir in mint. Brush melted mixture over cantaloupe skewers. Place skewers directly on grilling grate; grill for 4 to 6 minutes, turning to brown all sides. Serve with remaining sauce for dipping.

RISE AND SHINE!

The best time to water your lawn is between 4 and 6 a.m. This will give the ground enough time to absorb the water before the summer sun reaches full strength. In addition, high humidity and morning dew will add to the moisture, while low mid-day winds can blow the grass dry before evening.

Grilled Honeysuckle Pineapple

Makes 12 servings

1 whole fresh pineapple, peeled and cored

3 T. honey

¼ C. cherry brandy

2 tsp. lemon juice

Cut the pineapple into thick slices. In a large glass bowl, combine honey, cherry brandy and lemon juice. Add pineapple slices, stirring until well coated; cover and chill in refrigerator for 1 hour to marinate. Preheat an outdoor grill to medium heat and lightly oil the grate. Remove pineapple from bowl and discard any remaining marinade. Place pineapple slices directly on grilling grate for about 10 minutes, turning a few times, until pineapple is hot and caramelized.

Grilled Peaches & Cream

Makes 8 servings

4 whole fresh peaches,
  halved and pitted

1 T. vegetable oil

2 T. honey

1 C. cream cheese with
  honey and nuts

Preheat an outdoor grill to medium heat and lightly oil the grate. Brush the peach halves with a light coating of oil. Place peach halves directly on grilling grate, cut side down. Grill for 5 minutes. Turn peaches over; drizzle with a little honey. Place a dollop of cream cheese in the hollowed part of each peach half; grill for 2 to 3 minutes more or until filling is warm. Serve immediately.

FREEDOM TO FLY

In some countries, Flag Days are special holidays on which the national flag must be flown from public buildings as required by law. June 14th is Flag Day in the U.S.A. You can fly your American flag proudly and freely, while celebrating the fact that you are not forced to do so.

Strawberries Romanoff

Makes 6 servings

3 to 4 C. fresh strawberries
¼ C. sugar
1 C. heavy whipping cream

1 C. vanilla ice cream, softened
3 to 4 T. Cointreau or orange juice

Hull the strawberries, cutting any large berries in half. Place the strawberries in a bowl and sprinkle with sugar; chill in refrigerator. In a medium mixing bowl, beat heavy cream until stiff peaks form. Beat ice cream in a separate bowl until fluffy. Fold ice cream and Cointreau into whipped cream. Divide strawberries into six serving bowls; spoon cream mixture over top. Serve immediately.

Fruit n' Honey Pizza

Makes 12 servings

1 (16.5 oz.) tube refrigerated sugar cookie dough
2 T. honey
1 T. cornstarch
⅓ C. orange or apple juice
2 T. currant or apple jelly

1 C. sliced fresh strawberries
½ C. fresh blueberries or raspberries
1 fresh nectarine or peach, pitted and sliced
½ C. halved green or red grapes

Press dough evenly into a lightly greased 11″ or 12″ pizza pan. Bake crust for 12 to 14 minutes at 350° or until golden brown; let cool in pan on a wire rack. In a small saucepan over medium heat, combine honey and cornstarch. Stir in juice and jelly; heat until thickened and bubbly, stirring often. Remove from heat and let cool for 5 minutes without stirring. Spread half of the glaze over the cooled crust. Arrange fruit over crust then spoon remaining glaze over fruit. Chill for 30 minutes before cutting into slices and serving.

Triple Berry Trifle

Makes 8 to 10 servings

2 C. fresh or frozen
  raspberries

3 T. sugar

1 T. raspberry liqueur,
  light rum or orange juice

1 (3.4 oz.) pkg. instant
  vanilla pudding mix

2 C. milk

1 (8 oz.) pkg. cream
  cheese, softened

1 (6 oz.) carton vanilla
  yogurt

1 (10.75 oz.) loaf frozen
  pound cake, thawed
  and cubed

6 C. quartered fresh
  strawberries

2 C. fresh blueberries

In a blender or food processor, combine raspberries, sugar and liqueur; process until smooth. Pour into a bowl, cover and refrigerate. In a large bowl, whisk together pudding mix and milk for 2 minutes; set aside. In a large mixing bowl, beat cream cheese and yogurt until smooth. In a 2- to 3-quart trifle dish or glass bowl, layer ⅓ of the cake cubes. Top with ⅓ of the pudding mixture followed by ⅓ of the strawberries and blueberries and ⅓ of the cream cheese mixture; repeat layers two more times. Cover and chill. To serve, spoon raspberry sauce onto serving plates; top with a scoop of the trifle.

Glazed Pears

Makes 4 servings

⅓ C. apricot jam

¼ C. orange juice

4 fresh pears, halved,
  peeled and cored

1 C. whipped topping,
  divided

½ tsp. ground nutmeg,
  divided

Preheat oven to 350°. In a 9 x 13″ baking dish, combine jam and orange juice. Place pears in dish, cut side down, spooning some of the sauce over the pears. Bake for 25 to 30 minutes, or until tender. Place two pear halves in each of four dessert bowls. Top each with ¼ cup whipped topping and ⅛ teaspoon nutmeg.

LIGHT THE NIGHT

There are more than 1,900 known species of fireflies. The summer light show produced by fireflies is caused by a chemical in the beetles' bodies called luciferin. It reacts with oxygen to create light. Scientists believe the flashes produced by lightning bugs are used either to warn predators of their unpleasant taste or attract fireflies of the opposite sex.

Mint Crepes with Fruit Salad

Makes 6 servings

½ C. plus ⅓ C. sour cream, divided

2 large eggs

½ C. 1% or 2% milk

2 T. butter, melted

¾ C. flour

2 T. minced fresh mint

½ tsp. salt

2 C. chopped mixed fruit

2 tsp. sugar

In a medium mixing bowl, combine ½ cup sour cream, eggs, milk, butter, flour, mint and salt; mix until well combined. Heat a non-stick skillet or griddle to medium-high heat; spray lightly with non-stick cooking spray. Place about ¼ cup batter on the hot pan; swirl quickly to spread the batter into a thin circle. Cook crepe until cooked through; quickly flip over then remove to a piece of waxed paper. Repeat with remaining crepe batter. In a medium bowl, toss together mixed fruit, sugar and remaining ⅓ cup sour cream. Fill each crepe with some of the mixed fruit filling; fold over and serve. If desired, drizzle with one of the sauce recipes on page 72.

Orange Custard Sauce

Makes 2 cups

1 C. sugar

5 T. flour

Dash of salt

Zest of 1 orange

1 T. plus 2 tsp. lemon juice

½ C. orange juice

3 egg yolks

1 tsp. butter

1 C. heavy whipping cream

In a medium saucepan over low heat, combine sugar, flour and salt. Stir in orange zest, lemon juice, orange juice and egg yolks; blend well. Heat, stirring occasionally, until sauce is thickened and smooth. Stir in butter until melted. Remove from heat and let cool. In a medium mixing bowl, whip heavy cream until soft peaks form; fold into cooled sauce mixture. Serve custard sauce over pound cake or fresh summer fruit.

Strawberry Peach Sauce

Makes 2 cups

1 (15 oz.) can peach slices in syrup

¼ C. sugar

1 T. cornstarch

½ tsp. almond extract

4 to 6 large fresh strawberries, sliced

Drain and reserve syrup from peaches. In a medium saucepan, combine sugar and cornstarch; stir in reserved peach syrup. Cook, stirring occasionally, over medium-low heat until thickened. Stir in almond extract, peaches and strawberries. Continue to cook until heated through. Spoon sauce over pound cake, shortcake biscuits or angel food cake.

Lemon Berry Napoleon

Makes 5 servings

2 T. sugar

½ tsp. ground cardamom or cinnamon

4 sheets frozen phyllo dough

½ C. low-fat lemon yogurt

1 C. whipped topping

¾ C. fresh raspberries, blackberries or blueberries

Preheat oven to 350°. Lightly coat a baking sheet with non-stick cooking spray; set aside. In a small bowl, combine sugar and cardamom. Lightly coat top of phyllo sheets with cooking spray; sprinkle each with sugar and cardamom mixture. Layer the sheets on top of each other to make one stack. Cut the sheets into 4 strips and then cut each strip crosswise into 4 pieces to make 16 rectangles. Place stacked rectangles on prepared baking sheet; bake for 8 to 10 minutes, or until golden. Remove from oven and let cool. Meanwhile, combine lemon yogurt and whipped topping. To assemble desserts, spread lemon mixture over one side of each phyllo rectangle then sprinkle each with a few berries. Layer three covered rectangles on top of each other. Repeat to make five total desserts. There will be one extra phyllo rectangle in case of breakage.

PUT A LID ON IT

An outdoor gas grill is designed to cook food with the lid closed, similar to a kitchen oven. This helps food retain natural juices and keeps flare-ups to a minimum. In addition, heat reflected from the lid will help cook both sides of the food. It is acceptable to keep the lid open when grilling foods that require just a quick sear.

THE GREAT OUTDOORS

Summer is a great time to visit one of the many State Parks located in the United States. A State Park is an area of land preserved under the administration of state government for its natural beauty, historic interest or recreation. For a complete list of State Parks and historic sites, visit the National Park Service website at www.nps.gov.

Fruit Compote with Ice Cream

Makes 2 servings

1 C. cubed watermelon

½ C. diced apples

1 C. sliced honeydew melon

¾ C. seedless grapes

2 scoops ice cream, divided

6 fresh strawberries, sliced, divided

In a blender, combine watermelon, apples, melon and grapes; process until blended and smooth. If desired, pour mixture through a sieve to strain out any large pieces of fruit or peel. Pour compote into two serving bowls; top each with a scoop of ice cream and sliced strawberries.

Chilled Berry Soup

Makes 4 servings

1½ C. heavy whipping
  cream
1½ C. orange juice
½ C. strawberry or
  vanilla yogurt

1 T. sugar
1 C. sliced fresh
  strawberries, divided
Ground nutmeg

In a blender, combine heavy cream, orange juice, yogurt and sugar; process for 10 seconds. Divide soup evenly into four chilled bowls. Top each serving with ¼ cup strawberries and a dusting of nutmeg.

Raspberry Dessert Soup

Makes 4 servings

2 (10 oz.) pkgs. frozen
  raspberries in syrup,
  thawed
3 T. lemon juice
2 T. flour
1 C. vanilla ice cream

1 (11 oz.) can mandarin
  oranges in syrup
½ C. fresh raspberries
¼ C. water
Additional vanilla ice
  cream, optional

In a blender, combine thawed raspberries with syrup, lemon juice and flour; process until smooth. Pour mixture into a medium saucepan over medium heat; bring to a boil for 2 minutes. Remove from heat. Stir in 1 cup ice cream until melted then stir in oranges with syrup, fresh raspberries and water. Chill soup in refrigerator until cold. Ladle soup into four chilled bowls. If desired, top each serving with a small scoop of ice cream.

Peach Ambrosia

Makes 4 servings

2 C. sliced fresh peaches

1 medium banana, peeled and sliced

½ C. seedless red grapes

1 T. lemon juice

2 T. sugar

½ C. flaked coconut

In a medium bowl, combine peach slices, banana slices, grapes, lemon juice and sugar; toss until well combined. Chill in refrigerator for at least 1 hour. Before serving, fold in coconut. Spoon ambrosia into chilled dessert dishes and serve immediately.

Apple Brown Betty

Makes 8 to 10 servings

2 C. dry bread crumbs

1 C. brown sugar

1 tsp. ground cinnamon, divided

¼ tsp. ground cloves

10 C. sliced tart apples

⅓ C. butter, melted

⅓ C. applesauce

1½ tsp. sugar

Preheat oven to 350°. In a small bowl, combine bread crumbs, brown sugar, ½ teaspoon cinnamon and cloves; mix well and set aside. Spread half of the sliced apples across the bottom of a 9 x 13″ baking dish; top with half the bread crumb mixture. Repeat layers with remaining apples and bread crumb mixture. Pour melted butter over ingredients and cover with applesauce. Combine remaining ½ teaspoon cinnamon and sugar; sprinkle over applesauce. Bake for 1 hour or until apples are tender and mixture is bubbly.

Quick and Easy Watermelon Pie

Makes 8 servings

1 (12 oz.) can sweetened condensed milk

½ (8 oz.) tub whipped topping

¼ C. lime juice

2 C. watermelon balls

1 (9") prepared graham cracker pie crust

In a medium bowl, combine sweetened condensed milk and whipped topping; fold in lime juice and watermelon balls, reserving 5 balls for garnish. Pour filling into pie crust. Garnish with reserved watermelon balls. Chill in refrigerator for at least 2 hours before cutting into slices and serving.

POISONOUS PLANTS

If an outdoor hike is on your to-do list this summer, be prepared by identifying poisonous plants that may be growing in the area. Contact with plants such as poison ivy, poison oak or sumac may cause reactions and skin problems for some people. A common rule to remember is "leaves of three, let it be".

CHLORINE GOES GREEN

Visiting the local pool for a dip can be a great way to cool off in the summer, but chlorinated water can sometimes cause blonde or fair-colored hair to turn a light shade of green. Try washing hair with specialty shampoo made for swimmers. For a home remedy, dissolve two seltzer tablets in ½ cup water. Mix in 2 tablespoons of baby shampoo and wash hair as normal.

Strawberry Mousse Pie

Makes 8 servings

1 env. unflavored gelatin

2 T. water

3 egg whites

1 C. sugar

¼ C. lemon juice

1 C. whipped topping

2 (6 oz.) cartons strawberry yogurt

Dash of salt

1 (9″) prepared graham cracker pie crust

¼ C. sliced fresh strawberries

Sprinkle gelatin over water in a small microwave-safe bowl; let stand for 1 minute. Microwave for 15 seconds, stirring until gelatin is dissolved; let cool. In a medium mixing bowl, beat egg whites at high speed until stiff peaks form. In a medium saucepan over medium heat, combine sugar and lemon juice. Heat, stirring often, until sugar is melted. Increase heat to medium-high and cook, without stirring, until mixture registers at 240° on a candy thermometer. Pour syrup in a thin stream over egg whites while beating at medium speed until stiff peaks form, about 5 minutes. Beat in gelatin mixture. Fold in whipped topping, yogurt and salt. Spoon filling into pie crust; garnish with sliced strawberries. Cover and freeze for 4 hours.

Trio Berry Crisp

Makes 10 to 12 servings

1½ C. fresh blackberries
1½ C. fresh raspberries
1½ C. fresh blueberries
¼ C. sugar
2 C. flour

2 C. old-fashioned oats
1½ C. brown sugar
1 tsp. ground cinnamon
½ tsp. ground nutmeg
1½ C. butter

Preheat oven to 350°. In a large bowl, toss together blackberries, raspberries, blueberries and sugar; set aside. In a separate bowl, toss together flour, oats, brown sugar, cinnamon and nutmeg. Cut in butter with a pastry blender or two knives until mixture is crumbly. Press half of the crumbly mixture into the bottom of a 9 x 13" baking dish; cover with berry mixture. Sprinkle remaining crumbly mixture over berries. Bake for 30 to 40 minutes or until topping is golden brown and fruit is bubbly.

Berry Peach Pie

Makes 8 servings

4 C. peeled and sliced
  fresh peaches
1 C. fresh raspberries
¾ C. plus 1 T. sugar,
  divided
3 T. flour

1 tsp. ground cinnamon
1 (15 oz.) pkg.
  refrigerated
  pie crusts
2 T. butter, softened

Preheat oven to 400°. Place peaches and berries in a colander to drain off any liquid for 15 minutes. Transfer fruit to a large bowl. Add ¾ cup sugar, flour and cinnamon; toss until evenly coated. Place one pie crust layer in a 9″ pie pan; cut to size. Transfer fruit to pie pan. Dot butter over fruit; top with remaining crust layer and flute the edges to seal. Cut vents in top crust and sprinkle with remaining 1 tablespoon sugar. Bake for 45 minutes.

Blackberry Cobbler

Makes 8 servings

1 C. flour

1½ C. sugar, divided

1 tsp. baking powder

½ tsp. salt

6 T. cold butter

¼ C. boiling water

2 T. cornstarch

¼ C. cold water

1 T. lemon juice

4 C. fresh blackberries

Preheat oven to 400°. Line a baking sheet with aluminum foil; set aside. Combine flour, ½ cup sugar, baking powder and salt. Cut in butter with a pastry blender or two knives until mixture is crumbly. Stir in boiling water until mixture is evenly moist. In a large oven-safe skillet, combine cornstarch and cold water; mix in remaining 1 cup sugar, lemon juice and blackberries. Place skillet over medium-high heat and bring to a boil, stirring often. Drop dough by spoonfuls over the berry mixture. Place skillet on baking sheet; transfer to oven and bake cobbler for 25 minutes or until dough is golden brown.

Banana Cream Pie

Makes 8 servings

¾ C. sugar

⅓ C. flour

¼ tsp. salt

2 C. milk

3 egg yolks, beaten

2 T. butter

1¼ tsp. vanilla extract

1 (9") prepared pie crust, baked

4 bananas, peeled and sliced

Preheat oven to 350°. In a medium saucepan over medium heat, combine sugar, flour and salt. Add milk, stirring constantly, until mixture is bubbly. Continue stirring for 2 minutes. Remove from heat. Stir a small amount of the hot mixture into the beaten egg yolks; immediately stir egg yolk mixture into the remaining hot mixture. Return to heat for 2 more minutes, stirring constantly. Remove from heat; stir in butter and vanilla. Place the sliced bananas inside the baked pie crust; pour pudding mixture over top. Bake for 12 to 15 minutes. Chill for at least 1 hour before slicing.

Peach Shortcake

Makes 8 servings

1 (29 oz.) can peaches in light syrup

¼ C. sugar

2 C. flour

2 tsp. baking powder

½ C. butter or margarine

1 egg, beaten

⅔ C. 1% or 2% milk

Whipped topping

Preheat oven to 425°. Grease an 8″ round baking dish; set aside. Cut peaches into 1″ slices; set aside. In a medium bowl, combine sugar, flour and baking powder. Cut in butter with a pastry blender or two knives until mixture is crumbly. In a small bowl, combine egg and milk; stir into dry ingredients. Spread batter into prepared pan. Bake for 15 minutes or until a toothpick inserted in the center of the cake comes out clean. Remove from oven and cool for 15 minutes. Cut cake into 8 wedges. Cut each wedge into two layers. To assemble one serving, place the bottom half of a cake wedge on a dessert plate; top with about ½ cup peaches and 1 tablespoon peach syrup. Top with a dollop of whipped topping and top half of wedge. Top with another dollop of whipped topping and another spoonful of peach syrup. Repeat to make remaining servings.

THE CHERRY ON TOP

Cherry season peaks in June and July. During this small window of opportunity, pick up some fresh, sweet cherries from your local market. Generally, the darker the cherry, the sweeter the taste. Bing cherries are traditionally the darkest and sweetest, though Ranier and Queen Annes are also very sweet despite their yellowish-rose color. Look for firm, plump cherries with pliable green stems. Store them in a plastic bag in the refrigerator and devour them within three days.

Strawberry Rhubarb Jam

Makes 4 pints

5 C. thinly sliced fresh rhubarb

4 C. sugar

1 (3 oz.) box dry strawberry gelatin mix

In a large saucepan, combine rhubarb and sugar; let stand for 1 hour. Place saucepan over low heat; cover and bring to a rolling boil, stirring often. Remove from heat and stir in gelatin, mixing until gelatin is completely dissolved. Skim any foam from the top of the mixture. Pour jam into hot sterilized pint jars; cover with lids and process in a boiling water bath for 5 minutes according to canner manufacturer's instructions.

Triple Cherry Jam

Makes 6 pints

2 C. pitted light sweet cherries

2 C. pitted dark sweet cherries

2 C. pitted tart red cherries

6 C. sugar

Juice of 1 lemon

Place cherries in a food processor. Working in batches, pulse cherries until coarsely chopped. Pour chopped cherries into a large saucepan over medium-low heat; simmer for 5 minutes. Stir in sugar and lemon juice; simmer, stirring occasionally, until thickened, about 15 to 20 minutes. Skim any foam from the top of the mixture. Pour jam into hot sterilized pint jars; cover with lids and process in a boiling water bath for 5 minutes according to canner manufacturer's instructions.

Kid Pleasers

Melon Star Pops

Makes about 8 treats

1 watermelon   **Star cookie cutters**

Cut the melon into 1″ thick rounds. Use a star-shaped cookie cutter to cut a large star out of the melon flesh in each round. Insert a popsicle stick into each star. Place the stars on an aluminum foil-lined baking sheet; cover with another sheet of foil. Freeze for 1 hour or until firm.

Fig Pops

Makes 6 servings

6 fig fruit chewy cookies
6 T. peanut butter, divided

⅓ C. chopped peanuts, chocolate chips, shredded coconut or candy sprinkles

Insert a popsicle stick into each fig cookie. Spread about 1 tablespoon peanut butter over both sides of each cookie; sprinkle with peanuts, chocolate chips, coconut or sprinkles. Serve immediately.

Edible Campfires

Makes 1 serving

1 (12″) flour tortilla	1 T. chow mein noodles
1 red licorice rope	6 tootsie rolls
2 T. chopped peanuts	6 mini pretzel sticks
1 T. peanut butter	4 candy corns

Place the tortilla on a flat plate. Wrap the licorice rope around the edge of the tortilla to make a safety circle. Arrange the peanuts in a ring about halfway between the outer rim and the center of the tortilla to make the rock ring. Spread the peanut butter in a small circle in the center of the tortilla to make the fire base. Sprinkle the chow mein noodles over the peanut butter for kindling. Lay the tootsie rolls around the peanut butter as logs. Build a stick tepee with the pretzels over the kindling. Light the fire by placing the candy corns inside the pretzel stick tepee. Now put out the fire by eating it up!

ARE WE THERE YET?

Summer road trips, especially long ones, can be tough on kids. Plan your route with lots of stops along the way. This will make it easier and more adventurous for little ones. Remember to pack favorite books and soft toys to keep children occupied, and to help keep your attention on the road.

Green Leather

Makes 4 servings

1½ C. very ripe chopped kiwi	¼ C. light corn syrup

In a blender, combine chopped kiwi and corn syrup; process until very smooth. Cover a baking sheet with parchment paper; pour puree over top. Smooth the puree with a spatula so it covers the baking sheet evenly. The puree should be very thin. Place the baking sheet in the oven for 4 to 6 hours. Check every 30 minutes until the puree is pliable and has the feel of leather. It should not be wet or sticky. Remove the baking sheet from the oven and let it cool. Once the fruit leather is cool, roll it up in the parchment paper and cut into four pieces with kitchen shears. Store fruit leather in an airtight container until ready to serve.

Sprinkle Freeze Pops

Makes 8 popsicles

1 (3.9 oz.) box instant chocolate pudding mix	2½ C. chocolate milk 1 T. candy sprinkles

In a large bowl, combine chocolate pudding mix and chocolate milk; beat with a wire whisk for 2 minutes. Spoon some of the candy sprinkles into each popsicle mold. Spoon the chocolate pudding over the sprinkles in each mold. Transfer to the freezer; freeze until firm.

TEACH A MAN TO FISH.

Dust off that old fishing pole and take the kids fishing this summer! Research the lakes and rivers in your area, as well as the types of fish you might catch and the bait you should use. Pack up some sandwiches and cold drinks for the trip, and don't forget your fishing license.

Mock Melon

Makes 8 servings

1 honeydew melon

1 qt. raspberry sherbet

¼ C. semi-sweet chocolate chips

Refrigerate honeydew melon for 1 to 2 hours or until well chilled. Cut melon in half; scoop out and discard seeds. Pack the hollow part of each melon half full with raspberry sherbet. Slice each half into four wedges. Press chocolate chips into the sherbet on both sides of each wedge to look like watermelon seeds. Serve immediately.

Sand & Dirt Cups

Makes 8 cups

1 (3.4 oz.) box instant
vanilla pudding mix

4 C. cold milk, divided

1 (3.9 oz.) box instant
chocolate pudding mix

1 C. whipped topping

20 chocolate sandwich
cookies, crushed

16 gummy worms

In a large bowl, combine vanilla pudding mix and
2 cups milk; beat with a wire whisk for 2 minutes.
In a separate bowl, combine chocolate pudding
mix and remaining 2 cups milk; beat with a wire
whisk for 2 minutes. Let pudding mixtures stand
for 5 minutes. Gently fold ½ cup whipped topping
into each pudding mixture. Sprinkle 1 tablespoon
crushed cookies in the bottom of eight six-ounce
clear plastic cups; top each with a layer of ¼
cup vanilla pudding and another 1 tablespoon
cookie crumbs. Top each dessert cup with ¼ cup
chocolate pudding. Sprinkle remaining cookie
crumbs over top; refrigerate for 1 hour. Insert
two gummy worms into the pudding dessert just
prior to serving.

ANTS OR LADYBUGS

*For a quick and easy summer treat,
spread peanut butter over celery sticks.
Top each with a few raisins to make
"ants on a log", or use a few dried
cranberries in place of the raisins
to make "ladybugs on a log".
The kids will gobble them up!*

Eat Worms
Ice Cream Shake

Makes 1 serving

2 scoops cookies n' cream
  ice cream
½ C. milk

5 gummy worms
Whipped topping
Candy sprinkles

In a blender, combine ice cream, milk and gummy worms; process for 3 minutes. Pour blended mixture into a tall glass; top with whipped topping and sprinkles. Serve immediately.

Ladybug Treats

Makes 30 treats

½ C. creamy peanut
  butter
3 T. butter, softened
1 C. powdered sugar

1 C. red candy chips
15 black jelly beans
Black decorators' gel

In a medium bowl, combine peanut butter, butter and powdered sugar; mix until well blended. Roll the mixture into thirty 1" balls. Place the balls on a sheet of waxed paper; press down to gently flatten the bottoms. Melt the red candy chips according to package directions. Spoon the melted red candy over each ball, spreading with a knife until completely covered. Slice each jelly bean in half. Before the coating hardens, press one jelly bean half into the side of each ball to make the ladybug's head. Once the coating hardens, use black decorators' gel to add a stripe and spots to each bug.

ONE, TWO, THREE STRIKES YOU'RE OUT!

Baseball is the great American pastime of summer. Even if you don't live close to a major league ballpark, you can still take in a game at one of the many minor league fields scattered around the nation. Before you go, make sure the kids are ready for the seventh-inning stretch by teaching them the words to "Take Me Out to the Ball Game!"

Frozen Apple Cups

Makes 4 servings

1 C. applesauce	½ tsp. ground cinnamon
1 C. plain yogurt	½ tsp. ground nutmeg
1 tsp. vanilla extract	¼ tsp. ground cloves

In a medium bowl, combine applesauce, yogurt, vanilla, cinnamon, nutmeg and cloves; mix until well combined. Divide into four small cups; chill in refrigerator until ready to serve. If desired, the cups can be frozen in the freezer for 1 hour to make a frozen slushie treat.

Graham Sandwiches

Makes 4 sandwiches

½ C. peanut butter

1 large very ripe banana, peeled

¼ tsp. ground cinnamon

8 graham cracker squares

In a bowl, mash together peanut butter and banana with a fork until well blended. Stir in cinnamon. Spread mixture over four of the graham cracker squares; top with remaining squares to make four sandwiches.

Rainbow Snack Bars

Makes 12 servings

2½ C. broken pretzel sticks

2 C. crispy rice cereal

1½ C. M&Ms

½ C. peanuts

½ C. butter

⅓ C. peanut butter

5 C. pink marshmallows

In a large bowl, combine pretzels, cereal, M&Ms and peanuts; toss until well combined. In a large saucepan over low heat, melt butter and peanut butter; stir in marshmallows and heat until melted and smooth. Pour melted mixture over cereal mixture; stir quickly until evenly coated. Press mixture into a greased 9 x 13″ baking dish; chill in refrigerator until firm. Cut into squares and serve.

Critter Crunch

Makes 10 servings

1 C. animal crackers

1 C. teddy bear-shaped graham crackers

1 C. small pretzel twists

1 C. yogurt-covered raisins

1 C. M&Ms

10 flat-bottom ice cream cones

In a large bowl, combine animal crackers, graham crackers, pretzels, raisins and M&Ms; toss until well combined. Divide mixture evenly into ice cream cones. Serve immediately.

Sunshine Sandwiches

Makes 4 servings

¼ C. frozen orange juice concentrate, slightly thawed

½ C. peanut butter

8 slices white or wheat bread

In a medium bowl, combine orange juice concentrate and peanut butter; mix until well combined. Spread mixture over four slices of bread; top with remaining bread slices to make four sandwiches. Cut each sandwich into two triangles; serve immediately.

Life Preserver Treats

Makes 8 servings

1 (3 oz.) box berry blue
  gelatin mix

8 teddy bear-shaped
  graham crackers

8 gummy peach rings

Prepare gelatin with water according to package directions. Pour liquid evenly into 8 clear plastic cups; chill in refrigerator. Stick one graham cracker bear into each peach ring to look like an inflatable tube. Before the gelatin is completely set, stick the legs of each bear lightly into the surface of the gelatin so the tube sits on top of the gelatin and the bear looks like it is floating in water.

CURIOUS ABOUT CAMP?

If summer camp is in the plans for your kids, make sure they are prepared by knowing where they are going, for how long, and what the scheduled activities will be. This will make the transition a lot easier and probably get them excited for the adventure. Assure them a care package will be mailed, complete with goodies and letters from home.

Magical Potion Floats

Makes 8 servings

½ C. water

½ C. sugar

1 (.15 oz.) env. unsweetened
  orange drink mix

1 liter lemon-lime soda

8 scoops vanilla ice cream

In a large pitcher, combine water and sugar; stir in orange drink mix and lemon-lime soda. Place one scoop of ice cream in the bottom of 8 tall glasses. Slowly pour the orange drink mixture over top. Serve immediately with straws and spoons.

Grilled Ice Cream Sandwiches

Makes 1 serving

3 T. butter, softened

2 slices Texas toast

2 scoops peanut butter
  ice cream with fudge
  swirls

Spread butter over one side of each Texas toast slice. Place one slice, buttered-side down, in a nonstick pan over medium heat. Scoop ice cream onto one slice and top with the remaining slice of Texas toast, buttered-side up. After 3 minutes, flip the sandwich over to cook the other side for 2 minutes.

A BREATH OF FRESH AIR

*June is Great Outdoors Month
in recognition of the value of outdoor
recreational activity. Contact your Chamber
of Commerce or local newspaper for upcoming
outdoor activities and celebrations in the
month of June, such as National Clean
Beaches Week, National Trails Day, or the
Great American Backyard Campout.*

Sun-Baked S'mores

Makes 1 serving

2 graham cracker squares

1 T. semi-sweet chocolate chips

1 T. miniature marshmallows

Prepare this treat on a hot, sunny day. Place one graham cracker square in a foil pie plate. Sprinkle the chocolate chips and marshmallows over the graham cracker. Cover the pie plate with aluminum foil. Place the covered pie plate in a hot, sunny place. Check to see if the chocolate and marshmallows are melted after 10 minutes. Top with the remaining graham cracker square and enjoy!

PB Bumblebees

Makes 30 bumble bees

¼ C. butter or margarine, softened

1 C. creamy peanut butter

1 C. powdered sugar

1½ C. graham cracker crumbs

1 (1 oz.) square semi-sweet baking chocolate

⅓ C. sliced almonds

In a medium mixing bowl, beat butter, peanut butter and powdered sugar at medium speed until blended. Fold in graham cracker crumbs; mix well. Shape mixture into 1″ ovals to resemble the bee bodies; set on waxed paper. Melt baking chocolate according to package directions. Drizzle melted chocolate over bees to resemble bees' stripes. Insert two almonds into each bee to look like wings.

Mud Puddle Cake

Makes 16 servings

4 (1 oz.) squares unsweetened baking chocolate

¾ C. butter or margarine

2 C. sugar

3 eggs

1 tsp. vanilla extract

1 C. flour

1 (3.9 oz.) box instant chocolate pudding mix

1 C. cold milk

10 chocolate sandwich cookies, crushed

Gummy bugs and worms

Preheat oven to 350°. In a microwave-safe bowl, combine chocolate squares and butter; microwave for 2 minutes, stirring until melted. Blend in sugar, eggs and vanilla. Mix in flour. Spread batter into a 12″ greased pizza pan. Bake for 25 to 30 minutes, or until a toothpick inserted in center of brownies comes out with fudgy crumbs. Let brownies cool in pan on a wire rack. In a medium bowl, combine pudding mix and milk, stirring with a wire whisk until well blended; spread over brownies to within 1″ of the edge. Sprinkle crushed cookies over pudding and decorate with gummy bugs and worms.

Corn Dogs

Makes 16 servings

1 C. yellow cornmeal
1 C. flour
¼ tsp. salt
⅛ tsp. pepper
¼ C. sugar
4 tsp. baking powder

1 egg
1 C. milk
1 qt. vegetable oil for frying
2 (16 oz.) pkgs. beef frankfurters

In a medium bowl, combine cornmeal, flour, salt, pepper, sugar and baking powder; stir in egg and milk. Preheat oil in a deep saucepan over medium heat. Insert one wooden skewer into each frankfurter. Dip frankfurters in batter until well coated. Fry corn dogs in hot oil, a few at a time, for 8 to 10 minutes, or until lightly browned. Drain on paper towels and let cool slightly before serving.

TWO-TIMING TOWELS

If your beach towels are losing their luster, try giving them a second life by sewing them into beach tote bags. Make sure each bag is big enough to carry a rolled-up towel, sunscreen, sunglasses, a few water bottles, sandals and a cover-up. Attach a handle made out of sturdy material or rope.
If you're talented with a sewing machine, you could sew on a zippered pocket to hold loose change and lip balm with SPF protection.

BEYOND THE FIREWORKS

In the United States, the Fourth of July is a federal holiday commemorating the adoption of the Declaration of Independence. In addition to all the fireworks displays, parades, barbecues and picnics, Independence Day can also be a great opportunity to brush up on a little history. On July 4, 1776, America declared its independence from the Kingdom of Great Britain, and the first copy of the Declaration of Independence was released to the printer signed only by John Hancock, President of the Congress.

Fourth of July Cakes

Makes 24 cupcakes

1 (18.2 oz.) box white cake mix

½ C. dried cherries

2 C. small fresh blueberries

1 (8 oz.) pkg. cream cheese, softened

½ C. powdered sugar

1 tsp. vanilla extract

1 roll red fruit leather

Prepare cake batter as directed on package. Stir dried cherries into batter and spoon evenly into 24 paper-lined medium muffin cups. Place five blueberries on top of the batter in each cup; do not press into batter. Bake cupcakes as directed on package; remove from oven and let cool completely. In a medium bowl, beat cream cheese, powdered sugar and vanilla until smooth and creamy; spread over cooled cupcakes. Press nine blueberries, in three rows of three, in the top corner of each cupcake to look like stars on an American flag. Cut the fruit leather into strips that are ⅛″ wide by 2″ long. Drape fruit strips over remainder of each cupcake as the flags' stripes.

Strawberry Nibblers

Makes 8 snacks

8 vanilla wafer cookies
¼ C. whipped topping

4 fresh strawberries, halved

Place cookies on a serving plate. Top each with about 1½ teaspoons whipped topping. Place one strawberry half on top of each. Serve immediately.

Fruit Salsa with Cinnamon Chips

Makes 10 servings

2 kiwis, peeled and diced
2 Golden Delicious apples, peeled, cored and diced
2 C. fresh raspberries
3 C. sliced fresh strawberries

1 C. plus 2 T. sugar, divided
1 T. brown sugar
3 T. strawberry jam
10 (10") flour tortillas
1 T. cinnamon

In a large bowl, combine kiwis, apples, raspberries, strawberries, 2 tablespoons sugar, brown sugar and strawberry jam; mix until well combined and chill in refrigerator at least 15 minutes. Preheat oven to 350°. Coat one side of each tortilla with butter-flavored cooking spray. Cut tortillas into wedges and place on a large baking sheet. In a medium bowl, combine remaining 1 cup sugar and cinnamon. Sprinkle cinnamon mixture over chips and spray again with cooking spray. Bake for 8 to 10 minutes. Let chips cool for 15 minutes before serving with chilled fruit salsa.

Egg Bunnies

Makes 4 bunnies

4 hard-cooked eggs

3 stalks celery

1 T. shredded carrots

4 small broccoli florets

Peel the eggs. Slice a small piece off the wide end of each egg so it will stand on a plate. Cut the celery into eight ear shapes. Make two small slits with a knife on top of each egg; insert two celery ears into each egg. Stick a few shredded carrots into one side of each egg to look like whiskers. Make two small slits with a knife to place the eyes. Use small bits of carrot for the eye; stick them into the slits. Stick one small broccoli floret into the other end of each egg for the bushy tail. Serve immediately.

Party Poke Cake

Makes 12 to 15 servings

2 baked (9") round white cake layers, cooled

2 C. boiling water

2 (3 oz.) boxes dry cherry gelatin mix

1 (8 oz.) tub whipped topping

⅓ C. crushed chocolate sandwich cookies

With cake layers still in the pans, poke holes all over the surface of the cakes with a fork. In a medium bowl, combine boiling water and gelatin mix, stirring until gelatin is completely dissolved. Pour half the gelatin mix over each cake layer; refrigerate for 3 hours or overnight. Unmold cakes by dipping the bottom of the pans in warm water for 10 seconds then inverting onto a serving plate. Spread about 1 cup whipped topping over one cake layer; top with remaining cake layer. Frost top and side of cake with remaining whipped topping; refrigerate for 1 hour. Sprinkle crushed cookies on top of cake.

S'mores Brownies

Makes 36 brownies

20 graham cracker squares

¾ C. butter or margarine

4 (1 oz.) squares unsweetened baking chocolate

2 C. sugar

3 eggs

1 tsp. vanilla extract

1 C. flour

2½ C. miniature marshmallows

1 C. semi-sweet chocolate chunks

Preheat oven to 350°. Line a 9 x 13″ baking dish with aluminum foil, extending foil over edges of pan. Grease the foil. Place 15 graham cracker squares into bottom of pan, overlapping as needed. Break remaining 5 graham cracker squares into large pieces; set aside. In a microwave-safe bowl, heat butter until melted. Stir in chocolate until completely melted, microwaving in 20 second increments as needed. Stir in sugar, eggs and vanilla; mix well. Stir in flour until well combined; spread over graham cracker layer. Bake for 30 to 32 minutes, or until a toothpick inserted in center of brownies comes out with fudgy crumbs. Sprinkle marshmallows and chocolate chunks over brownies. Return to oven for 3 to 5 minutes or until marshmallows begin to puff; press reserved graham cracker pieces into marshmallows. Let brownies cool in pan. Lift brownies out of pan by pulling on foil; cut into 36 small bars.

SPLISH AND SPLASH

Create lasting summer memories by cranking on the lawn sprinklers and letting the kids splash around in their swimsuits. Don't worry about messing up the lawn or tracking grass into the house – this is what summer is all about!

Banana Split Cake

Makes 12 servings

1 (16 oz.) pkg. vanilla
  wafers, crushed

1 C. butter or margarine,
  melted

1 (8 oz.) pkg. cream
  cheese, softened

2 C. powdered sugar

1 (20 oz.) can crushed
  pineapple, drained

6 bananas, peeled
  and sliced

1 (12 oz.) tub whipped
  topping

¼ C. chopped walnuts

12 maraschino cherries

In a medium bowl, combine crushed wafers and butter; press into the bottom of a 9 x 13″ baking dish. In a separate bowl, beat together cream cheese and powdered sugar until light and fluffy; spread over crust layer. Spoon crushed pineapple over cream cheese layer and top with banana slices. Cover with whipped topping and sprinkle with chopped walnuts and cherries. Refrigerate until ready to serve.

Baseball Cakes

Makes 24 cupcakes

1 (18.2 oz.) box white
  cake mix

10 chocolate sandwich
  cookies, crushed

2 C. whipped topping

Red decorators' gel

Prepare cake batter as directed on package. Stir crushed cookies into batter and spoon evenly into 24 paper-lined medium muffin cups. Bake cupcakes as directed on package; remove from oven and let cool completely. Frost cupcakes with whipped topping. Draw stitching on top of cakes with red decorators' gel to look like baseballs. Store in refrigerator until ready to serve.

Crowd Favorites

Strawberry Spinach Salad

Makes 8 servings

2 bunches fresh spinach, rinsed and torn

4 C. sliced fresh strawberries

½ C. vegetable oil

¼ C. white wine vinegar

½ C. sugar

¼ tsp. paprika

2 T. sesame seeds

1 T. poppy seeds

In a large bowl, toss together spinach and strawberries. In a medium bowl, whisk together oil, vinegar, sugar, paprika, sesame seeds and poppy seeds. Pour dressing over spinach and strawberries; toss until evenly coated. Serve immediately.

BLT Basil Salad

Makes 4 servings

½ lb. bacon

½ C. mayonnaise

2 T. red wine vinegar

¼ C. finely chopped fresh basil

4 slices French bread, cut into ½" pieces

1 tsp. salt

1 tsp. pepper

1 T. vegetable oil

1 lb. romaine lettuce, rinsed and torn

2 C. quartered cherry tomatoes

Cook bacon in a large skillet over medium-high heat until evenly browned; drain skillet, reserving 2 tablespoons of the drippings. Crumble bacon and set aside. In a small bowl, whisk together reserved bacon drippings, mayonnaise, vinegar and basil; cover and let stand at room temperature. In the same skillet over medium heat, toss bread pieces with salt and pepper; drizzle with oil and continue to heat, stirring often, until golden brown. In a large bowl, combine lettuce, tomatoes, bacon and croutons; pour dressing over top and toss well. Serve immediately.

Pretzel Surprise Salad

Makes 8 serving

1½ C. crushed pretzels

1 C. plus 4½ T. sugar, divided

¾ C. butter, melted

2 (8 oz.) pkgs. cream cheese, softened

1 (8 oz.) tub whipped topping

1 (6 oz.) pkg. dry strawberry gelatin mix

2 C. boiling water

2 C. sliced fresh strawberries or 1 (16 oz.) pkg. frozen strawberries

Preheat oven to 350°. In a large bowl, combine pretzels, 4½ tablespoons sugar and butter; mix well and press into the bottom of a 9 x 13″ baking dish. Bake for 10 minutes, or until lightly toasted; set aside to cool. In a medium bowl, beat remaining 1 cup sugar with cream cheese until smooth; fold in whipped topping. Spread evenly over cool crust; refrigerate for 30 minutes. In a separate bowl, combine gelatin mix and boiling water; stir in strawberries, mixing until gelatin is completely dissolved. Pour over cream cheese layer; return to refrigerator for 1 hour.

PAMPERING PEDICURE

When warm weather hits, it's time for sandals and open-toed shoes. If you're not ready to show off your little piggies, try this home remedy. In a medium bowl, combine 1½ cups brown sugar, 1 teaspoon vanilla extract and ½ cup olive oil. Mix until a paste forms. Apply a thick coating to your feet, massaging soles and heels. After 10 minutes, wash feet with warm water and pat dry with a clean towel. Apply some foot moisturizer and you're ready to roll!

Angel Food Strawberry Dessert

Makes 10 to 12 servings

1 (10") prepared angel food cake

2 (8 oz.) pkgs. cream cheese, softened

1 C. sugar

1 (8 oz.) tub whipped topping

4 C. sliced fresh strawberries

1 (18 oz.) jar strawberry glaze

Crumble the cake into a 9 x 13" baking dish; press down to make a flat layer. Combine cream cheese and sugar, mixing until light and fluffy; fold in whipped topping. Spread over cake layer. In a medium bowl, combine strawberries and glaze, mixing until coated; spread over cream cheese layer. Chill at least 1 hour before serving.

Berry Artisan Pies

Makes 2 desserts, 24 servings

1½ tsp. sugar

½ tsp. ground cinnamon

1 (15 oz.) pkg. refrigerated pie crusts

2½ C. half-n-half

1 (5.2 oz.) box instant vanilla pudding mix

2 C. whipped topping

2 C. sliced fresh strawberries

2 C. fresh blueberries

1 C. fresh raspberries

Preheat oven to 450°. Combine sugar and cinnamon; set aside. Unroll crusts on separate baking sheets; sprinkle each with sugar and cinnamon mixture. Prick pie crusts with a fork. Bake for 8 to 10 minutes, or until lightly golden; set aside to cool. Beat half-n-half and pudding mix with a wire whisk until blended; gently fold in whipped topping and chill in refrigerator until ready to serve. Just prior to serving, spread pudding mixture over pie crusts. Top each with 1 cup strawberries, 1 cup blueberries and ½ cup raspberries. Cut into slices.

BEWARE OF RARE

Grilled meats are one of summer's great pleasures, but it is important to cook all meats to a safe temperature. The USDA recommends fully cooking meats to ensure all bacteria is destroyed. Hamburgers and ribs should be cooked to 160°F or until the center is no longer pink and the juices run clear. Cook ground poultry to 165°F and poultry parts to 180°F.

Peach Muffins

Makes 12 muffins

1 C. quick-cooking oats
1 C. buttermilk
¼ C. vegetable oil
2 T. molasses
1 tsp. vanilla extract
1 egg
1¼ C. flour
¼ C. diced fresh peaches

¾ C. chopped pecans, optional
¼ C. brown sugar
1½ tsp. ground cinnamon
1 tsp. baking soda
1 tsp. baking powder
½ tsp. salt

Preheat oven to 400°. In a large bowl, combine oats and buttermilk. Mix in vegetable oil, molasses, vanilla and egg with a fork, mixing until well combined. Stir in flour, peaches, pecans, brown sugar, cinnamon, baking soda, baking powder and salt. Lightly grease the bottom of twelve muffin cups. Divide batter evenly into cups. Bake for 20 minutes or until a toothpick inserted in center of muffins comes out clean.

Pineapple Party Dip

Makes about 2½ cups

1 (8 oz.) pkg. cream
  cheese, softened

⅔ C. evaporated milk

¾ tsp. vanilla extract

½ C. shredded coconut

1 small pineapple,
  peeled, cored and diced
  or 1 (8 oz.) can crushed
  pineapple, drained

In a medium bowl, beat cream cheese until softened. Mix in evaporated milk and vanilla, stirring until smooth. Stir in coconut and pineapple. Chill in refrigerator until ready to serve. Serve as a dip for crackers or fresh fruit.

NATURAL SURROUNDINGS

To capture the whimsy of an outdoor garden party, decorate with the environment's natural palette. Fill a glass bowl with lemons and limes for a burst of brightness, or fill dessert cups to the brim with pink and red cherries. For a softer look, arrange fresh flowers in tin drinking cups and place a bouquet at each table setting.

Grasshopper Frozen Dessert

Makes 8 servings

1 C. crushed chocolate wafer cookies

¼ C. butter, melted

1 (7 oz.) jar marshmallow cream

2 T. crème de menthe liqueur

2 T. crème de cacao liqueur

Green food coloring

1 C. heavy whipping cream

Set aside 1 tablespoon cookie crumbs. Toss remaining cookie crumbs with butter in a medium bowl; press into the bottom of an 8˝ square baking dish. In a small mixing bowl, combine marshmallow cream, crème de menthe and crème de cacao. Stir in drops of food coloring until mixture reaches desired shade of green; beat with an electric mixer at medium speed until light and fluffy. In a separate mixing bowl, beat heavy cream until soft peaks form; fold into marshmallow mixture. Spoon over crumb layer; sprinkle with reserved cookie crumbs. Freeze for 8 hours or overnight. Cut into squares and serve.

Sparkling Peach Dessert Cups

Makes 4 servings

4 ripe fresh peaches

1 C. raspberry sorbet

½ C. sparkling white wine, chilled

4 T. chopped almonds, toasted

Cut each peach in half and discard the pit. Dice the peach flesh and divide into four wine or dessert glasses. Top each with one scoop of sorbet. Pour 2 tablespoons sparkling wine over the sorbet in each glass; top each with 1 tablespoon almonds.

GET FIRED UP

Whether you are fond of the stack method or the pyramid method, here are a few handy tips to ensure your next campfire will burn safely and brightly. Start by clearing the area of all debris and avoid building a fire in areas with overhanging branches. If a fire ring is not available, construct one out of rocks. Stack your wood, tinder and kindling in separate piles away from the fire, and never use green, wet or freshly cut wood. Start by burning some tinder and then build up kindling and wood, making sure not to drown out the flame.

Chocolate Milk Mousse

Makes 8 desserts

1¼ C. heavy whipping cream

⅓ C. sugar

3 T. cornstarch

1 C. chocolate milk

½ C. water

1 egg yolk, beaten

1¾ C. semi-sweet chocolate chips

1 tsp. vanilla extract

Beat heavy cream at medium speed until stiff peaks form; set aside. In a medium saucepan over medium-high heat, combine sugar and cornstarch; stir in chocolate milk and water. Heat, stirring often, until just boiling. Beat egg yolk in a small bowl; stir in some of the hot mixture then add to the saucepan. Bring to a boil for 1 minute, stirring constantly. Remove from heat; stir in chocolate chips and vanilla until chocolate is melted. Transfer mixture to a small metal bowl; set inside a large bowl filled with ice. Fold in ¾ of the whipped cream. Spoon mousse into eight dessert glasses. Top each with a dollop of the remaining whipped cream; serve immediately.

Frozen Peanut Butter Bars

Makes 12 to 16 servings

1 (18 oz.) tube
  refrigerated chocolate
  chip cookie dough
1 C. creamy peanut
  butter

1 C. light corn syrup
½ gallon peanut butter
  ice cream with fudge
  swirls
1 C. fudge sauce

Press cookie dough into the bottom of an ungreased 9 x 13″ baking dish. Bake for 12 to 15 minutes or until crust is golden brown; set aside to cool. In a medium bowl, combine peanut butter and corn syrup; mix well and set aside. Cut ice cream into 1″ wide slices; arrange over cooled crust, cutting as needed to fit. Smooth ice cream with a spatula; freeze for 30 minutes. Spread peanut butter mixture over ice cream layer; return to freezer for another 30 minutes. To serve, cut into rectangles. Drizzle each serving with some of the fudge sauce.

Ice Cream Cobbler Cake

Makes 9 servings

1 (9 oz.) box single-layer
  yellow cake mix
2 C. vanilla ice cream
2 T. chopped pecans,
  optional

½ tsp. ground cinnamon
1 (21 oz.) can cherry pie
  filling

Preheat oven to 350°. Sprinkle cake mix in the bottom of a greased 2-quart oval baking dish. Top with tablespoonfuls of vanilla ice cream; sprinkle with pecans and cinnamon. Spoon pie filling over top. Bake for 55 to 60 minutes or until the edges begin to brown and center is set. Let cool for 30 minutes before serving. Serve warm.

Peach Pound Cake

Makes 16 servings

1 C. butter or margarine,
  softened
2 C. sugar
4 eggs
1 tsp. vanilla extract

3 C. flour, divided
1 tsp. baking powder
½ tsp. salt
2 C. chopped fresh
  peaches

Preheat oven to 325°. Grease a 10″ tube pan with butter and coat with sugar; set aside. Cream together butter and sugar until light and fluffy. Stir in eggs, one at a time, beating well after each addition; mix in vanilla. In a separate bowl, sift together 2¾ cups flour, baking powder and salt; gradually stir into creamed mixture. Coat peaches with remaining ¼ cup flour; fold into batter. Spread batter evenly into prepared pan. Bake for 60 to 70 minutes or until a toothpick inserted in center of cake comes out clean. Let cake cool completely before inverting on a wire rack.

Rhubarb Cake

Makes 18 servings

¾ C. butter or
  margarine, softened,
  divided
1½ C. sugar
1 egg
1 tsp. vanilla extract
2 C. plus 1 T. flour,
  divided

1 tsp. baking soda
¼ tsp. salt
1 C. buttermilk
2 C. chopped fresh
  rhubarb
2 tsp. ground cinnamon
1 C. brown sugar

Preheat oven to 350°. In a large bowl, cream together ½ cup butter and sugar; mix in egg and vanilla. In a separate bowl, combine 2 cups flour, baking soda and salt; alternately add to creamed mixture with buttermilk. Toss rhubarb with remaining 1 tablespoon flour; fold into batter. Spread batter smoothly into a greased 9 x 13″ baking dish. In a medium bowl, combine remaining ¼ cup butter, cinnamon and brown sugar; sprinkle over batter. Bake for 45 minutes.

Coconut Toffee Freeze

Makes 12 servings

1 C. flaked coconut, toasted

2 C. crushed buttery round crackers

¼ C. butter, melted

¼ C. unsweetened applesauce

3 C. skim or 1% milk

2 (3.4 oz.) boxes instant coconut cream or vanilla pudding mix

1 qt. toffee crunch ice cream

1 (12 oz.) tub whipped topping

1 C. chocolate-covered toffee bits

Preheat oven to 350°. In a medium bowl, combine coconut, cracker crumbs, butter and applesauce; mix well and press into the bottom of a 9 x 13″ baking dish. Bake crust layer for 11 to 13 minutes or until the edges begin to brown; set aside to cool. In a large bowl, whisk together milk and pudding mix for 2 minutes. Stir in ice cream and half of the whipped topping, mixing to break up the ice cream; spread over crust layer and freeze for 2 hours. Before serving, spread dessert with remaining whipped topping and sprinkle with toffee bits.

BEGINNER'S LESSON

Looking for a reason to pick up a new hobby? July is National Tennis Month and August is National Golf Month. If you're new to the court or course, start by renting equipment for an afternoon and taking a beginner's lesson. That way, you can find out if it's the activity for you before making a bigger investment of time and money.

Neapolitan Sandwich Cake

Makes 10 to 12 servings

10 Neapolitan ice cream
  sandwiches
1 (12 oz.) tub whipped
  topping

2 C. chocolate syrup
½ C. chopped peanuts

Layer ice cream sandwiches in the bottom of a 9 x 13″ baking dish, cutting as necessary to fit. Spread whipped topping over sandwiches; top with chocolate syrup and peanuts. Chill in freezer until ready to serve.

Strawberry Yogurt Cake

Makes 8 to 10 servings

1 (18.25 oz.) box white
  cake mix
¾ C. water
⅓ C. vegetable oil
3 egg whites
2 (6 oz.) cartons
  strawberry yogurt,
  divided

1 (8 oz.) pkg. cream
  cheese, softened
Powdered sugar
10 fresh strawberries,
  thinly sliced

Preheat oven to 350°. Grease the bottom and sides of two 8″ or 9″ round cake pans. In a large bowl, combine cake mix, water, oil, egg whites and one carton of yogurt; beat on medium speed for 2 minutes. Pour batter into prepared pans. Bake for 30 to 35 minutes or until a toothpick inserted in center of cakes comes out clean; set aside to cool. Meanwhile, combine remaining carton of yogurt and cream cheese. Stir in powdered sugar until frosting reaches desired consistency. Spread some of the frosting over one cooled cake layer; top with other layer. Frost top and sides of cake with remaining frosting; garnish with strawberries.

A REPELLING REMEDY

*This summer, ward off pesky mosquitoes
with an effective natural remedy that
will protect you from both biting bugs and
harsh chemicals. Place two ounces of distilled
water in a deep mixing bowl. Using a wire
whisk, beat water quickly while slowly
drizzling two ounces of olive oil into the bowl.
Once all the oil is added, stir in about
20 drops of citronella essential oil.
Use this mixture as a lotion to rub on arms,
legs and other exposed skin areas.*

Candy Bar Cake

Makes 16 servings

1 (18.2 oz.) box dark
  chocolate cake mix

5 C. butter pecan
  ice cream

½ C. caramel topping

1 C. marshmallow cream

Prepare and bake cake mix according to package
directions for two 8″ or 9″ round layers. Let cakes
cool to room temperature. Place one cake layer,
top side down, on a serving plate; top with ice
cream and drizzle with caramel topping. Spread
marshmallow cream on bottom side of remaining
cake layer; place, marshmallow-side down, on top
of caramel. Freeze cake for 2 hours before cutting
into slices and serving.

Key Lime Pie

Makes 8 servings

1 T. unflavored gelatin

⅓ C. fresh lime juice
or Key lime juice

1 C. boiling water

¼ C. sugar

1 (12 oz.) can evaporated
milk, chilled

¼ C. cold water

1 (3.4 oz.) box instant
vanilla pudding mix

Pinch of lime zest

1 (9″) prepared graham
cracker pie crust

In a blender, combine gelatin and lime juice; process for 10 seconds. Let sit for 1 minute then stir in boiling water; cover and blend on high speed until gelatin is completely dissolved. Add sugar, evaporated milk, cold water, pudding mix and lime zest; cover and blend until smooth. Chill mixture in refrigerator for 20 minutes; spoon into prepared pie crust. Chill pie in refrigerator for 4 hours before cutting into slices and serving.

Bananas in Rum Sauce

Makes 4 servings

2 T. butter

¼ C. brown sugar

4 medium ripe bananas,
peeled and split
lengthwise

2 C. vanilla ice cream

2 T. light rum

Melt butter in a large skillet over low heat; stir in brown sugar until completely melted. Add bananas and sauté for 10 minutes or until just tender, turning once. Divide bananas evenly into four serving dishes, spooning sauce from skillet over bananas. Top bananas in each dish with a few scoops of the ice cream and a drizzle of rum.

No-Bake Cookies n' Cream Cheesecake

Makes 10 to 12 servings

3½ C. finely crushed chocolate sandwich cookies, divided

6 T. butter or margarine, softened

¼ C. cold water

1 env. unflavored gelatin

1 (8 oz.) pkg. cream cheese, softened

½ C. sugar

¾ C. milk

1 C. heavy whipping cream

In a medium bowl, combine 2 cups crushed cookies and butter; mix well and press into the bottom of a 9″ springform pan. In a medium saucepan over medium heat, combine cold water and gelatin; heat, stirring often, until gelatin is completely dissolved. In a separate bowl, combine cream cheese and sugar at medium speed until well blended; gradually stir in gelatin mixture and milk, mixing well. Chill mixture in refrigerator until thickened but not set. Beat heavy cream at medium speed until stiff peaks form; fold into chilled mixture. Set aside 1½ cups of the cream cheese mixture. Pour remaining cream cheese mixture over crust layer. Top with remaining 1½ cups crushed cookies and reserved cream cheese mixture.

RELAX: CHECK!

Start your summer by writing down a list of all the things you want to do. Include everything from books you want to read to fix-it-up projects to people and places you want to visit. Once your list is long and complete, cross off half of the things you wrote down. Remember that summer is a time to revive your mind and body by relaxing. Try to mix in some free time along with crossing a few things off your to-do list.

Index

Frozen Favorites

Slushies, Smoothies & Coolers

Summer Snacks

Fabulous Fruit

Kid Pleasers

Crowd Favorites